The Art of Making Elegant Wood Boxes

The Art of Making Elegant Wood Boxes

Tony Lydgate

A Sterling\Chapelle Book
Sterling Publishing Co., Inc. New York

For all whose love for wood has led them
to turn their hands to sharing its beauty.

Research, text and artist coordination / Tony Lydgate

Concept, design and production / Chapelle Designs
Terrece Beesley and Jo Packham, owners

Trice Boerens
Tina Annette Brady
Sandra Durbin Chapman
Holly Fuller
Kristi Glissmeyer
Susan Jorgensen
Margaret Shields Marti
Jackie McCowen
Barbara Milburn
Lisa Miles
Pamela Randall
Jennifer Roberts
Florence Stacey
Nancy Whitley
Gloria Zirkel

Computer diagrams / Brian McComb

Photography / Ryne Hazen

With thanks and appreciation to / Penelope Hammond, Layton, Utah
Kaylene's Furniture, Ogden, Utah
Jo Packham, Ogden, Utah
Dean Perkins, Ogden, Utah
Edie Stockstill, Salt Lake City, Utah

Library of Congress Cataloging-in-Publication Data

Lydgate, Tony.
The art of making elegant wood boxes / by Tony Lydgate.
p. cm.
Includes index.
ISBN 0-8069-8838-X
1. Woodwork. 2. Wooden boxes. I. Title.
TT180.L93 1992
745.593—dc20 92–38556
CIP

10 9 8 7 6 5 4 3 2 1

Published by Sterling Publishing Company, Inc.
387 Park Avenue South, New York, N.Y. 10016
Produced by Chapelle Ltd.
P.O. Box 9252, Newgate Station, Ogden, Utah 84409

Distributed in Canada by Sterling Publishing
c/o Canadian Manda Group, P.O. Box 920, Station U
Toronto, Ontario, Canada M8Z 6P9
Distributed in Great Britain and Europe by Cassell PL
Villiers House, 41/47 Strand, London WC2N 5JE, Eng
Distributed in Australia by Capricorn Link Ltd.
P.O. Box 665, Lane Cove, NSW 2066
Printed and Bound in Hong Kong

Sterling ISBN 0-8069-8838-X

Contents

General Instructions

General Instructions

INTRODUCTION

An unopened box is only a vessel, a package, a container. Yet, because the contents are unknown, a box has about it a powerful air of mystery. It lures with the promise that something desirable lies concealed inside.

This book is a celebration of boxes that invites woodworkers of every skill level, from beginner to master, to share in the delights of creating this most intriguing and sublime of objects. Twenty-three box projects are included, each with exploded diagrams and complete how-to building instructions. A Gallery section showcases thirteen masterpieces from America's leading contemporary box-makers.

All projects are designed to be made in the home workshop. They are intended solely for personal use, not for commercial sale or manufacture.

The following pages provide an introduction to the why and how of box-making. Beginners will benefit from the explanations of some tricks of the trade; the skilled will enjoy seeing which of their many secrets are explained and which are left to be discovered through experience.

– Tony Lydgate

1. GETTING STARTED

Follow this basic rule to success in box-making: start where you are, with what you have, and make a box. Any box. Then make another box. Continue making boxes, and looking back at your first efforts will in time become pleasantly embarrassing. When wood-working magazines and tool catalogs arrive in the mail, filled with fabulous machinery and shiny gadgets, remember that Chippendale, Hepplewhite and the other master British and European cabinetmakers had no power tools, no carbide bits, no aluminum oxide abrasives. Their splendid work was created by judicious and persistent application of the very attributes you have in such abundance: determination and a firm belief in your own way of doing things.

Whether making a box exactly as shown, using the plans as a basis for variations, or setting out to create something completely new, begin by visualizing the finished product. Does it fit the function it will serve? How well will its moveable parts operate and how long will they last? Most important, enjoy imagining how wonderful the finished piece will look, reflecting the individual vision and style of its maker.

TOOLS

The right tools produce the best results in the most efficient manner. The many milling operations involved in box-making may be performed in different ways, including entirely by hand, but the power tools listed below will do the job more quickly and easily.

Table Saw

The box-maker's basic tool, this machine rips, crosscuts, rabbets, resaws, dadoes, bevels, slots, trims, miters and angles. A 10" blade diameter is the most practical size and heavier-duty models are preferable because they are more accurate, especially for repeated cuts. A sturdy fence and adjustable miter fence are essential accessories. Saw blades should be carbide tipped and kept sharp. Kerf width and the number and type of teeth vary according to the particular cut to be made. Saw blades will accumulate resin, especially when milling dense hardwoods; after each hour of use clean them with spray-on oven cleaner.

6" x 48" Belt Sander

Sanding objects with flat surfaces is easiest on a stationary belt sander and 6" x 48" is a convenient and widely available size. Coarse grit belts such as 30x and 60x are useful for removing large areas of excess wood and/or glue. Medium grit belts such as 120x and 150x shape, round, bevel, and accomplish essential intermediate steps in the overall sanding process. Polishing belts, described in more detail in Section 4, produce a perfect mirror finish at the final stage of making the piece.

The table saw and belt sander are the box-maker's two workhorse tools. In addition, it is useful to own or have access to a **drill press**, **band saw**, **shaper** (or **router** with **router table**), **joiner**, **planer**, **thickness sander**, and **orbital** or **vibrator sander**. These tools simplify many operations, saving time. However, the skilled box-maker will use ingenuity to develop an alternative technique if necessary; and this often leads to fresh designs and discoveries. In a perfectly-equipped shop where machines do most of the thinking, such serendipity is not so readily encountered.

Another important source of happy accidents is the errors that even the most skilled craftsmen inevitably make. It is said that the mark of a true master in any field is the ability to fix mistakes. To this add that a good box-maker views a mistake not as a vexing obstacle, but as a creative opportunity.

2. WOODS

WOOD SELECTION

The secret of magnificent boxes lies in selecting magnificent woods. The challenge of harmonizing the numberless patterns and colors of wood and the joy of spending working days with such beauty inspired many of the box-makers in this book to become woodworkers.

Although each project includes a list of the woods used, creating unique and unusual wood combinations is part of the fun of box-making. If supplies of a listed species are unobtainable, substitute whatever is available locally. One often overlooked source for interesting woods is the backyard. Many local species not commercially harvested yield beautiful lumber. Moreover, grain patterns such as burl, birdseye, crotch, curly or fiddle-back appear in these species as frequently as in more familiar woods. Revealing these glories, which otherwise would remain hidden forever beneath branch and bark, is the woodworker's privilege and sacred duty.

Although wood in any form may be used as a starting point, the most useful box-making lumber is boards of 1" or 2" thickness. Look for interesting color, grain, or figuring, even if not uniformly distributed through the entire board. Unlike furniture, box-making does not require huge quantities of lumber; a small burl, knot, or flash of figuring may be perfect for a box lid or drawer front. Use the remaining plain board for drawer sides, trays or other parts not in need of drama.

Purchase tropical hardwoods from a source that practices sustainable-yield forest management. Rainforests, source of most tropical woods, are a vital global resource.

Boards are often milled before being offered for sale. A planer removes the rough exterior, allowing the natural color and grain to show more clearly, and one edge is ripped straight. Though this assists the buyer, it also reduces available thickness and may cause difficulty in getting certain parts out of a given board. Also keep in mind that those piles of shavings on the sawmill floor are money; surfaced lumber costs more than rough lumber.

For these reasons, buy lumber rough whenever possible. Box-makers develop an ability to "read" the grain of a roughsawn board. This permits detection of figure that a casual observer may miss, besides providing thicker stock to work with back in the shop.

The cost of a project depends on the materials used. Fine hardwoods vary widely in price, with the most expensive being very costly indeed. But, taking into consideration the many hours of painstaking labor invested in the finished piece, using the best-looking species regardless of cost is worthwhile and rewarding.

SWELLING AND SHRINKING

Although harvested lumber does not continue to grow, it remains a living material, for its pores breathe in response to the surrounding climate. Many an otherwise splendid box has been brought to grief by the natural tendency of wood to shrink or swell. Experienced woodworkers employ several approaches to cope with this problem.

First and most important, use only lumber that has been properly kiln- or air-dried. Second, mill side walls and related parts thinner, rather than thicker. Where appropriate, utilize floating panels in which the edges of a solid piece are captured in over-deep dadoes in the surrounding frame. For massive parts, use finger joints, pins, dovetails, splines, slipfeathers or other types of joinery that provide mechanical reinforcement for the adhesive bond. Third, use veneers over a substrate of thin cross-grain laminates — commonly known as plywood — wherever possible.

USING PLYWOOD

Because it is used in so many time- and cost-saving ways, plywood has developed a bad reputation and some believe it has no place in fine woodworking. Nothing could be further from the truth.

Found in the tombs of the Egyptian pharaohs, plywood is among the most ancient of all woodworking innovations. The dimensional stability it offers is indispensable for coaxing wood to span larger areas while still remaining on its best behavior. The bottoms of many boxes and trays in this book are of veneer plywoods, especially when they are to be lined, because it is simply the best material for the job: strong, stable, lightweight, and efficient in its use of both labor and materials.

3. MILLING

Whether done by hand or with the most sophisticated machinery, all milling operations have the same purpose: to produce precisely dimensioned parts. From the simplest butt joint to the most complex dovetail, parts fit together best — and stay together — only if carefully and properly milled in the beginning.

PREPARING THE STOCK

Once lumber for box parts has been selected and cut to rough size or "blanked out", give each piece as flat a face as possible, using the belt sander or joiner. Since the irregular grain of many highly-figured woods leads to chipping or tear-out, the belt sander is often the most appropriate choice. With one face flat, parts can be accurately ripped to thickness.

Allow for finish sanding by adding a hair to the final dimension and rip on the table saw, using a pushstick. If the finished piece is to be taller than about 3", which is the maximum cutting height of a 10" table saw blade, two passes will be needed to complete the rip cut to thickness.

Parts are then trimmed to width, again adding a hair to the dimension to allow for edge sanding. Then run the parts through an abrasive planer (thickness sander), if available. This tool produces uniform and precisely dimensioned parts and accomplishes the initial step in the sanding process by accurately laying down parallel grooves of equal depth on the surface of the wood.

Parts deliberately milled slightly thicker and wider can be quickly brought down to precise final dimension by repeated passes through the abrasive planer. Dimensioned and sanded parts are now ready for the slots, rabbets, dadoes or holes that will later facilitate assembly of bottoms, rails, dowels, sides and hinge pins.

Milling small pieces of wood can be awkward; parts that will be shorter than about 9" should be prepared "two up" whenever practical. Lumber for the jewelry box on page

26, for example, with finished exterior dimensions of 7½" x 12", would begin as two pieces about 20" long. Perform all dimensioning, slotting, and preassembly sanding operations on this longer, easier-to-handle stock, crosscutting to final size prior to mitering.

In box-making, more than in any other type of woodworking, milling and assembly alternate in the sequence of steps leading to the final product.

Dimensioned parts are glued together, then the resulting assembly must be re-milled in preparation for yet another assembly. This back-and-forth process may be repeated a number of times.

THE MITER JOINT

The miter is one of the most versatile types of joinery. The resulting joint is neat in appearance, does not show endgrain and can be easily reinforced with splines or slipfeathers. The secret to successful miters is accurate milling. The angles of both the table saw blade and the miter fence must be accurately set and precisely maintained. For miters on stock less than 3" wide, set the miter fence at the required angle and stand the piece on its edge for milling.

For miters on wider stock, set the table saw blade at the appropriate angle, return the miter fence to 90° and lay the piece on its face. In both cases, make trial cuts on scrap pieces first to be sure miter settings are as accurate as available tools will permit.

SLIPFEATHERS

The slipfeathers used in several of the projects in this book (e.g., pages 30, 36, and 78) are triangular wedges glued into saw kerfs milled horizontally in the corners of a box, lid or other part.

Slipfeathers mechanically reinforce the adhesive bond in a joint, also providing a strong visual element. They are made by passing a part or assembly over the table saw blade on a carrier block. The work sits on edge in a 90° V-groove cut into this block (see diagram below).

In its simplest form, a slipfeather block can be made from a 12" length of two-by-four. The number, depth and placement of any slipfeathers varies with the design and the kerf width determines their thickness.

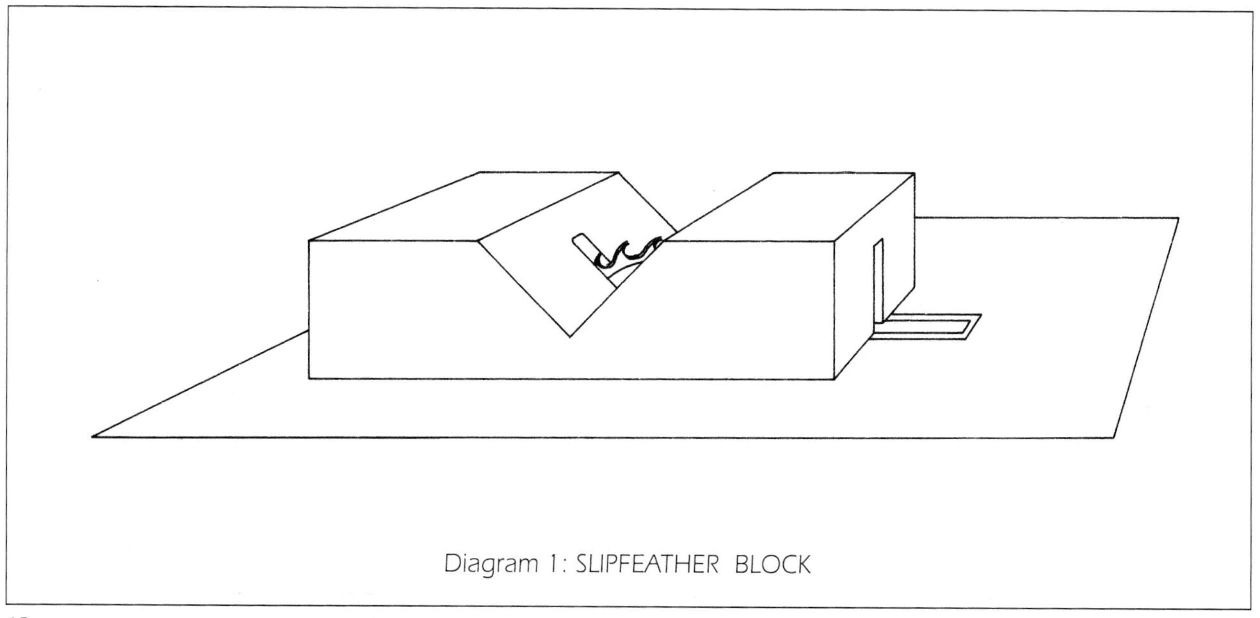

Diagram 1: SLIPFEATHER BLOCK

TRAYS AND DIVIDERS

A velvet-lined tray is an important finishing feature of any project designed for jewelry, collectibles or similar small treasures. An elegant but practical version, adaptable to a variety of sizes and shapes, is illustrated below.

Stock for sides is dadoed to receive the tray bottom, then milled at the ends of the long sides for a rabbet joint. Miters may also be used but the rabbet joint ensures more precise control of the tray's final size; this is important if more than one tray at a time is produced. Use 1/8" veneer plywood with one hardwood face for the bottom, which will later be lined with a velvet pad.

The finished tray may be divided into any number of compartments. For dividers, cut saw kerfs into the underside of a rectangular rail that exactly fits inside the tray. Small divider strips 1/8" thick, with top edges rounded on the sander, are then glued into the kerfs.

Oil the entire assembly, let dry and place in its tray atop the velvet pad. Pins driven partway through the sides of the tray into the ends of the long rail hold the divider firmly in place. These may be countersunk, the holes filled with small dowels and sanded flush.

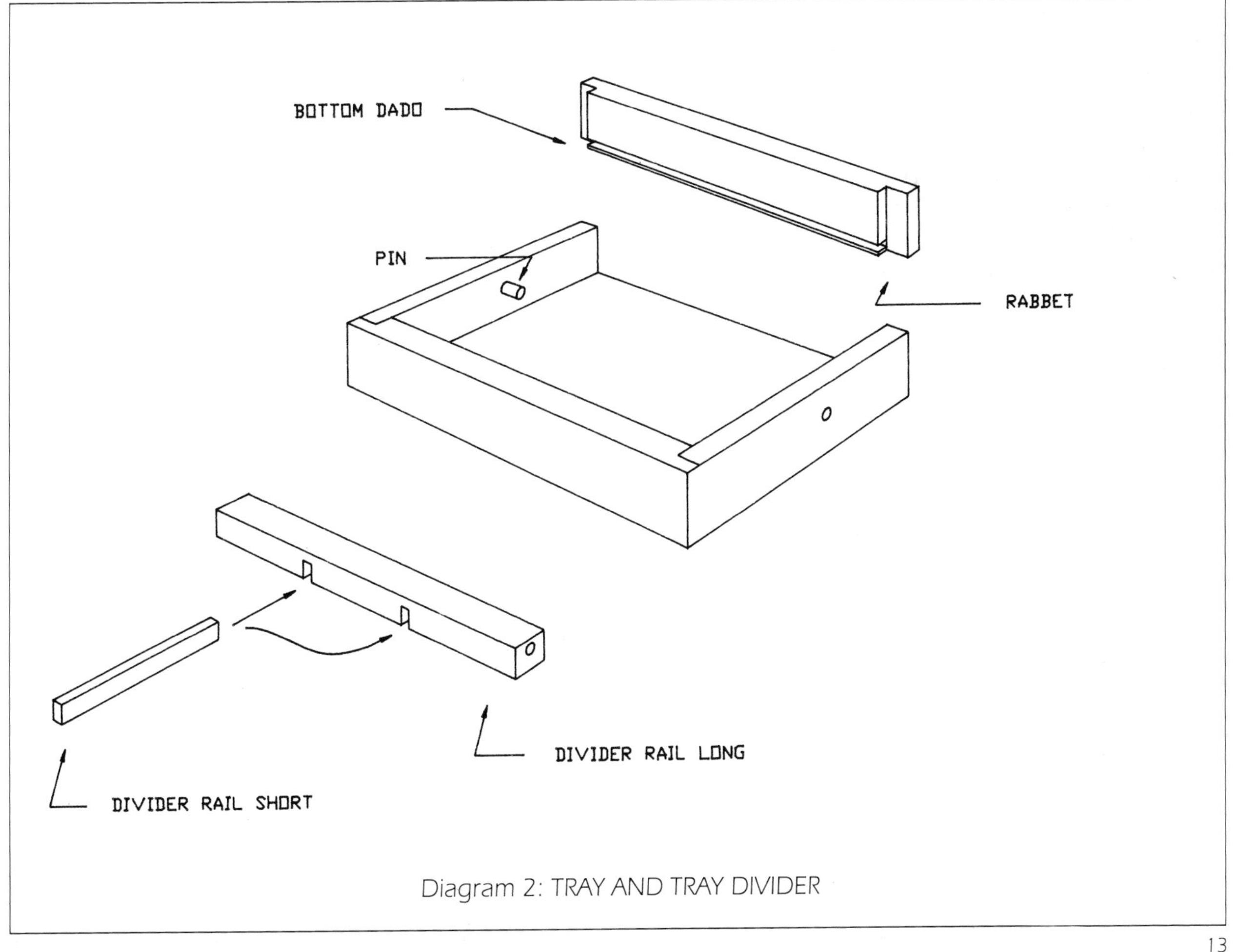

Diagram 2: TRAY AND TRAY DIVIDER

4. SANDING

The most important element in the look of a finished box is the shape and feel of its finished surfaces; sanding is the operation that produces them. The boxes in this book utilize abrasive treatments for the shaping of forms, for roundovers and eased radii, general flat face smoothing and the final pre-oiling step called polishing.

POLISHING

To abrade is to scratch; abrasives such as sandpaper do precisely that. Consisting of a jumble of tiny rocks glued to a paper or cloth backing, abrasives carve a pattern of grooves into the wood, like furrows plowed into a field. A belt sander creates multiple parallel grooves of uniform depth. The depth is determined by the grit rating of the abrasive; as this rating increases, groove depth decreases. A perfect finish is produced by repeated sanding with progressively finer grits, making the parallel grooves shallower and shallower until they finally disappear.

Following an orderly declension of grits is absolutely vital. Too broad a leap, such as from coarse to very fine with nothing in between, will prove unsatisfactory. An attempt to remove 60x scratches with a 220x abrasive will simply produce well sanded scratches; 220x rocks are too small to obliterate grooves made by 60x rocks. When the 60x is followed by a 120x, then a 180x and lastly a "polishing" belt, however, the result is a mirror-smooth surface.

Standard belts for the 6" x 48" sander are available up to about 180x but even these leave

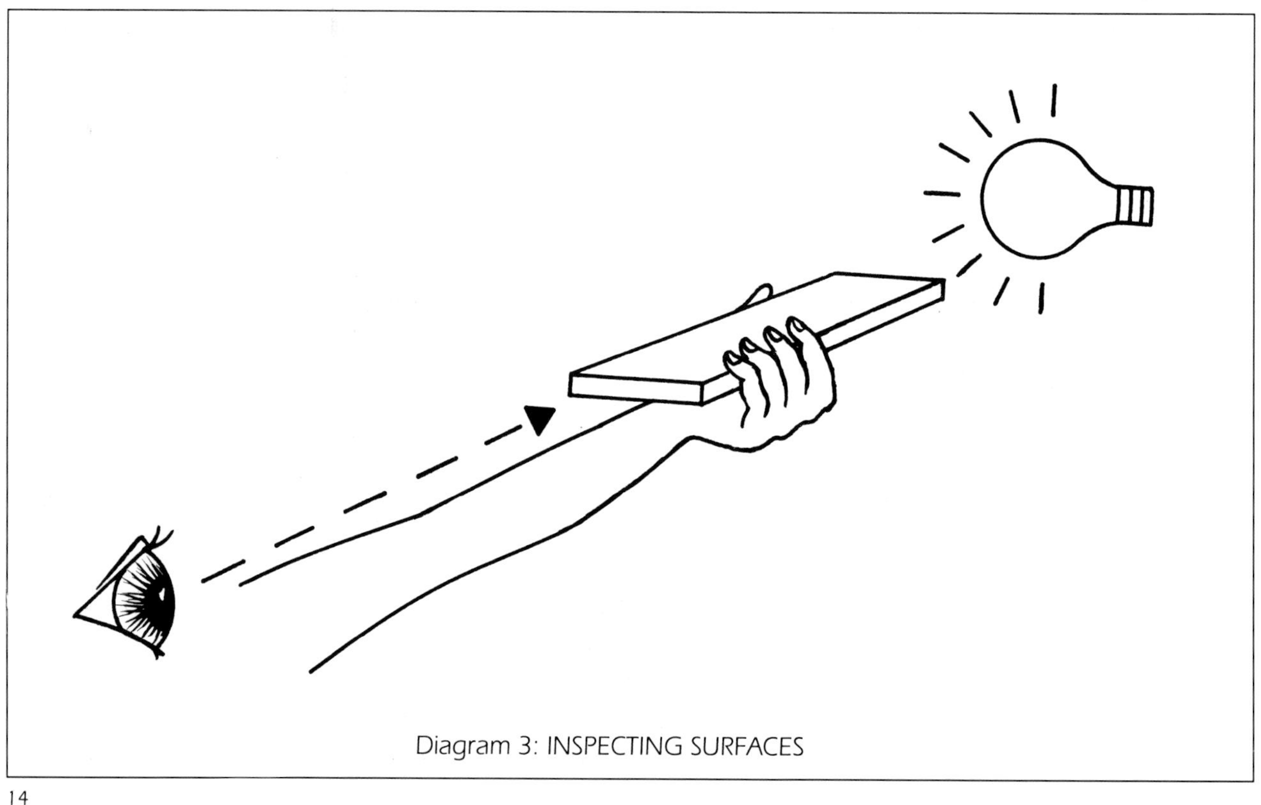

Diagram 3: INSPECTING SURFACES

scratches that will show as furry patches on the completed box. The solution is a polishing belt.

To create one, make a well-worn 120x or 150x belt even less abrasive by further dulling its already rounded rocks. Either apply wax to the belt or carefully and repeatedly use it to sand a piece of heavy, resinous hardwood or soft metal.

A polishing belt is ready if no visible dust comes off the end of the belt when it is in use. Although it requires some experimentation to produce, a good polishing belt can have the effect of 300x to 400x and is ideal as the last in a series of progressively finer abrasive treatments.

Curved or irregular shapes cannot be polished on the flat platen of the belt sander. The best means of bringing such surfaces to the desired mirror finish is hand or orbital sanding. Caution must be used with orbital sanders as they occasionally leave circular scratches when crossing the grain. They may also produce unwanted roundovers as the pad passes over the edge of a piece.

Hand-sanding is always the best method for all irregular shapes; unlike belts, sheet sandpaper is available in grits up to at least 600x. The more irregular the shape and the harder the wood, the more time and effort will be needed to achieve a good finish.

Whatever method is used, frequently interrupt the sanding process to check the work with the eye, that best of all tools. The following procedure is useful for determining the exact condition of a surface.

Hold the part palm up in one hand and extend the arm. Select a window, skylight or lightbulb as a light source and make a straight line between the source, the eye and the surface to be inspected (see diagram, opposite page).

Adjust the position of the hand until the angles are correct and the light will pick up every detail of the surface, even the tiniest scratches. When this extended-arm inspection no longer reveals any defects, the polishing process is complete and the piece is ready for its liquid finish.

OTHER SANDING OPERATIONS

Some box parts must literally be sculpted from a block of wood. A moving abrasive belt, drum or sleeve is often the most effective way to accomplish this, especially if the shape is irregular or curved. Routers, carving tools, shapers and band saws may also be used but these leave rough surfaces that require additional sanding prior to finish. Moreover, using any cutting tool with figured hardwoods risks chipping and tear-out. Skill at shaping small parts on the stationary belt sander is important in box-making; fortunately, only patience and practice are needed to acquire it.

At some point, parts, assemblies, carcasses, lids and the like must be freed of accumulated tool marks, glue, newspaper, clamp dents, tape adhesive, pencil notations and other unwanted elements marring exterior surfaces. In most instances, the belt sander is quite adequate for this operation.

The grit selected depends on the material to be removed. A coarse belt, such as 60x, is ideal for grinding off stubs of slipfeathers and the dried glue around them. In contrast, for a flat box part with only minor imperfections, a sharp 150x belt is the best choice. It will not only remove the minimum surface necessary in the shortest time, but also prepare the surface for the next higher grit.

Many boxes have flat sides meeting at crisp mitered corners. However, when these corners are too crisp, their edges are too sharp for comfortable handling. More important, a too-sharp edge will inevitably collect tiny dings and dents, every one of them clearly visible. To prevent this, the sharp edges of a box should be lightly sanded or "edge-killed" by hand prior to final finish.

In some designs, the top edges of a box carcass are to be rounded over. The desired curve is not a true radius but somewhere half-way between that and a 90° angle. It is referred to as an "eased radius". The invisible-hinge jewelry box on page 26 is an example. This edge treatment makes the finished product more durable and more pleasing to the eye. It is produced on the belt sander by holding the box firmly in both hands and rocking the edge back and forth over the moving belt, with the grain parallel to the direction of rotation, until the desired degree of rounding is achieved.

Where a true radius is desired, such as in the Marquetry Box on page 67, the belt sander quickly and efficiently removes the slight tool marks that even the sharpest carbide bit will leave. There is generally no need to sand outside surfaces prior to assembly, especially when they are flat. Sanding after glue-up will smooth the outside surfaces, remove excess glue, grind slipfeathers or laminates flush and correct any irregularities of squareness or form.

5. ASSEMBLY

The instructions for most of the boxes in this book call for sanding inside surfaces to finish-ready condition prior to assembly.

Because doing so afterwards is usually impossible, these parts are "polished" before glue-up, as described in the previous section.

Before gluing up an assembly, go through a dry run, putting all the parts together first without the adhesive. This is particularly important with more complex assemblies. The dry run not only tests for fit, but also rehearses the assembly process, alerting the box-maker to problems that may arise during time-sensitive glue-up. Another useful practice is the testing of every assembly for square, plumb or true immediately after gluing when adjustments are still possible.

ADHESIVES

Aliphatic or "white" glue, a convenient and economical adhesive, is appropriate for most projects. Epoxy or various types of waterproof glue may also be used. Glue should always completely cover surfaces to be joined. In general, too much glue is preferable to too little; a slight excess is evidence that there is sufficient glue to hold the joint securely. But this excess will be rock-hard by the next day and difficult to remove without marring the carefully polished surface. To avoid this, let the glue dry to the consistency of stiff chewing gum. Depending on the type of glue and temperature, this requires an hour or so. The excess may now be safely removed with a sharp chisel.

To prevent unwanted bonding – such as gluing the box to the work table or the laminate strips to the clamping jig – use a single sheet of newspaper as a liner or separator. Despite its thinness, the newspaper will not be penetrated by the glue and when dry, everything will neatly sand off.

GOOP

No matter how carefully made, the joints in any project may show tiny gaps or voids which must be filled prior to final sanding. The colors of commercial wood fillers are never quite right, especially when unusual or homegrown woods are used. A custom-made filler or "goop" is a better alternative. Apply a scrap piece of the wood to be matched to the belt sander and carefully collect the resulting fine dust. Mix this with glue, then force the mixture into the gaps with the flat blade of an old chisel.

Experiment to determine the proper consistency. If the proportion of glue to dust is too great, the result will be runny and dry as a glue line, which will not take a satisfactory finish. If there is too little glue and too much dust, the goop will be difficult to apply and will dry rough.

CLAMPING

C-clamps or other mechanical screw-type clamps are essential where substantial pressure is required, as when gluing laminate strips. However, they are not widely used in box-making because the small scale of most box assemblies does not require that much force. Clamping holds the faces of a joint firmly together until the adhesive sets; for boxes, the most effective clamping is done with paper or cloth tape.

TAPING A JEWELRY BOX CARCASS

To assemble the mitered jewelry box on page 26, for example, the following sequence would be used. Lay the two shorter sides, inside faces down, on the work table. Tear off four pieces of 2"-wide cloth tape, each as long as the part is wide (in this case that is about 3"). Apply tape to each mitered edge so that 1" of the tape's width adheres firmly to the wood and the other inch overhangs. Apply glue to the miter faces of the two untaped long sides and to the kerf dadoes on all four sides. Insert the bottom in one long side, add a short side, adjust the parts until the miters meet and fold the loose portion of the tape tightly around the corner onto the long side. Repeat with the remaining two sides. Tape should be tightly stretched for maximum effectiveness. Test the assembly for right angles with a square and correct as needed. If a corner does not align properly, the tape can be peeled off, the joint adjusted and the tape reapplied or more tape added. Tape should be removed as soon as the glue has set, for some brands become increasingly difficult to remove over time.

6. FINISHING

Obtaining a beautiful finish has almost nothing to do with the product being used and almost everything to do with the preparation of the surface to which it is applied. The silken, liquid look of a perfect finish, with its illusion of depth, is the result of time and effort, not obscure ingredients or arcane compounds. Once the right wood has been selected, all that is required to bring out its natural beauty is proper surface preparation.

The common but lamentable custom of drowning such splendid woods as mahogany, walnut, cherry or oak in a brown or reddish stain may be justifiable where inappropriate or poorly matched woods must be used, but it has no place in elegant box-making.

VARNISH AND LACQUER VS. PENETRATING OIL

Two types of clear finish are used on the projects in this book: penetrating oil, which soaks into the wood and then hardens, and varnish or lacquer which lies on top of it.

Varnish is the finish of choice in projects where contact with liquids is likely, such as those on pages 40 and 96. Polyurethane is the most common varnish; apply at least three coats, following manufacturer's instructions. Lacquer's quick drying time makes it easier to work with than varnish but it is neither as durable nor as water-resistant. Furthermore, its thinner consistency means that more coats are needed to produce a satisfactory finish.

Penetrating oil finishes will show off dramatic figure and grain patterns better than multiple coats of lacquer or varnish, which cover the surface and tend to fill the pores of the wood. Oil finishes are relatively simple to apply and have the advantage of not requiring a dust-free environment. Oil can be applied with a cloth, then rubbed in with fine steel wool.

When the surface is dry, use steel wool again to smooth it. The final step is application of an appropriate wax, which is then rubbed to high lustre by hand or with a buffing wheel.

7. FINAL TOUCHES

Among the many pleasures of the box, one of the greatest is the sense of anticipation as it is opened. The mystery of the interior is part of the essence, so make the interior as pleasing as the exterior whenever possible. Lining the bottom with a rich material such as velvet or suede adds to the visual excitement and also provides a practical method of protecting both the box and its treasured contents.

A simple procedure for linings is to wrap the lining material over pieces of poster board or mat board that have been cut about 1/16" smaller than the space to be lined. Exact dimensions of the mat board will vary with the thickness of the lining material. Cut the lining material 1/2" wider all around than the mat board; attach with spray adhesive. For neat corners, use a sharp blade to cut off triangles as shown in the diagram. Apply more adhesive, then fold the lining material to the back. The completed pad should jam in place tightly enough to stay put, but not so tightly that the mat board buckles.

Finally, an electric engraver or other tool may be used to add the box-maker's signature or mark, the date, the woods used and an inscription or dedication.

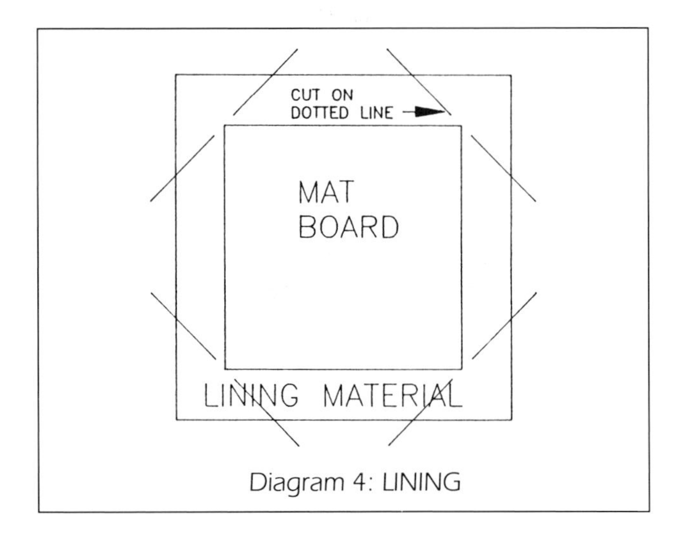

Diagram 4: LINING

Despite all precautions, nothing is immune to the ravages of time. Finishes dull, colors fade, woods dry out, parts shift, adhesives weaken and cracks open and close with the passing seasons. These do not detract from the beauty of a box but rather certify that it was created by human hands using natural materials.

8. SAFETY

Woodworking is inherently dangerous. The raw material itself can be heavy, sharp-edged and splintery and the tools used to fabricate it are all potentially lethal. These factors, combined with noxious dust, harmful chemicals, high noise levels and large quantities of electricity, produce an environment in which disfiguring, crippling or even fatal injury can occur in dozens of unforeseen ways. To operate a safe wood shop, always keep this in mind.

The risk of injury can never be completely removed, but it can be reduced to an acceptable level by strict observation of certain guidelines.

1. For safe operation of all tools, fully understand and adhere to the manufacturer's instructions.

2. Never allow fingers to come near any moving blade or cutter. Use a push stick.

3. Always wear a respirator or dust mask in the shop. Always wear ear and eye protection when using power tools.

4. Wear appropriate clothing. A heavy work apron will protect the mid-section from the occasional table saw kick-back. A dropped chisel hurts less on a protected toe than on a bare one; do not wear sandals in the shop.

5. Never perform any operation without being satisfied that you understand it and are comfortable with it.

6. Keep your mind on the work. Do not allow your attention to wander, especially when performing any repetitive operations.

7. Never work when tired, in a hurry, or simply not in the mood to work. It is better to stop, or find something to do outside the shop for a while. Return refreshed and in the proper frame of mind.

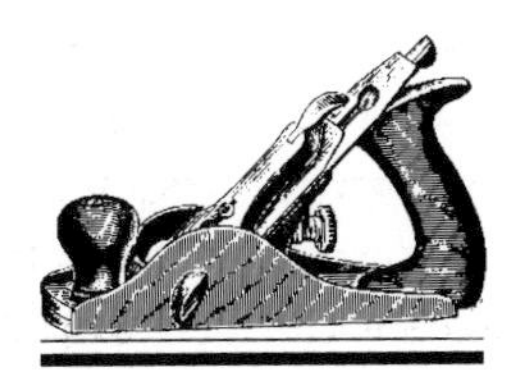

Wood Shop

Creating Elegant Wood Boxes

Versatility

A Three-drawer Jewelry Chest by Tony Lydgate

A box with drawers is among the most useful and versatile of all containers. This box's particular design makes efficient use of space and has an elegant finished appearance despite its relatively simple construction. Three drawers are shown in the photograph, but the design is easily adapted to two, four, five or more.

Drawer dividers may be customized to suit the contents: jewelry, as shown, collectibles, chessmen, mineral specimens or dry flies. The possibilities are endless.

WOOD

California walnut is a hybrid created by grafting fruiting stock from one type of walnut onto root stock of a different variety. The resulting lumber frequently has a richer look than traditional black walnut, with subtle undertones of orange and blue. The pernambuco handles on this chest dramatically highlight the walnut used. Pernambuco is an extremely dense hardwood traditionally used only for violin bows. This design succeeds in either dark or light woods. The detailing may offer a striking contrast, as in the pictured version, or a subtle one.

MILLING

Because of the relatively large size of this piece, starting with flat stock of uniform thickness is of particular importance. If possible, take the top and sides from a single piece of wood, so that the grain flows in a continuous pattern. After these parts have been ripped to width and crosscut to length, use a dado blade to mill the large rabbet in the sides, then rabbet the rear inside edge of all three parts to take the 1/4" plywood back. Finally, mill the 1/4" dado in the sides for the drawer tracks. Be careful of the fragile foot left after the bottom dado is milled.

The joinery in this chest is "screw and glue", a technique used in boat building and harpsichord making that is extremely strong. If preferred, use dovetails or finger joints instead.

Test the plug size and drill bit diameter before boring the plug holes to make sure they match. The shallow dado in the inside of the 1/4" plywood back, into which the rear edge of the bottom is glued, is important for the overall strength of the piece.

ASSEMBLY

Glue the two small filler blocks into the bottom dado and finish-sand the outer face of the back plywood. Lay out screws, an electric drill with a bit slightly smaller than the diameter of the screws for tapping the screwholes into the butt ends of the top, and a screwdriver (an electric one makes life much easier). Apply a bead of glue to the top rabbet and bottom dado of both sides. Standing the parts on their front edges, assemble the top and sides and insert the bottom. Run a bead of glue along the rabbet on the rear of the carcass, as well as in the dado on the inside of the back, and put the back in place. Gripping the carcass firmly, turn it to its upright position on the work table, making sure the front edges of the top and sides are perfectly flush. Drill tapper holes into the top through the three screwholes on one side of the carcass, insert screws and tighten. Repeat with the other side. Turn the box onto its front edge and fasten the plywood back with a staple gun, small brads or screws. Keep fasteners close to the edge of the plywood so they will not show after the facings are glued on. These facings should be fine-sanded and rounded on the inside

edges before applying; use masking tape to hold them while the glue dries. Plugs are then dipped in glue and tapped into the holes and drawer tracks are glued in. Drawer construction is conventional. Dovetails or finger joints may be substituted. Handles are stronger and easier to apply if milled with a 1/8" keel that is glued into a saw kerf slot milled on the drawer front before assembly. Dividers may be made as shown or modified to suit drawer contents.

FINISHING

Once the carcass is glued and dry, sand off excess material from plugs and facings, which should be milled a little longer and wider than needed, and rough-shape the shoulder radius on a 6"x 48" belt sander. If preferred, prior to assembly these shoulders can be radiused using a round-over bit on a shaper. Drawers should be sanded for smooth fit. Final sanding is done with a small vibrator at 220x or higher grit.

MATERIALS: Versatility, A Three-drawer Chest

Part	Description	Dimensions	Quantity
A	Top	3/4" x 7¾" x 15¾"	1
B	Side	3/4" x 7¾" x 8"	2
C	Back	1/4" x 7¼" x 15¾"	1
D	Bottom	1/4" x 7" x 15¾"	1
E	Drawer rail	1/4" x 1/2" x 7½"	4
F	Edge facing	1/8" x 13/16" x 17"	4
G	Filler block	1/4" x 1/4" x 5/8"	2
H	Drawer front	3/4" x 2¼" x 15¼"	3
I	Drawer side	3/8" x 2" x 7⅜"	6
J	Drawer back	3/8" x 2" x 14"	3
K	Drawer bottom	1/4" x 6$\frac{13}{16}$" x 14"	3
L	Pull	3/8" x 5/8" x 11"	3
M	Cardboard	6¼" x 13$\frac{7}{16}$"	3
N	Velvet	7¼" x 15"	3
O	Divider - long	3/8" x 3/4" x 14½"	As req'd
P	Divider - short	1/8" x 3/8" x 6½"	As req'd

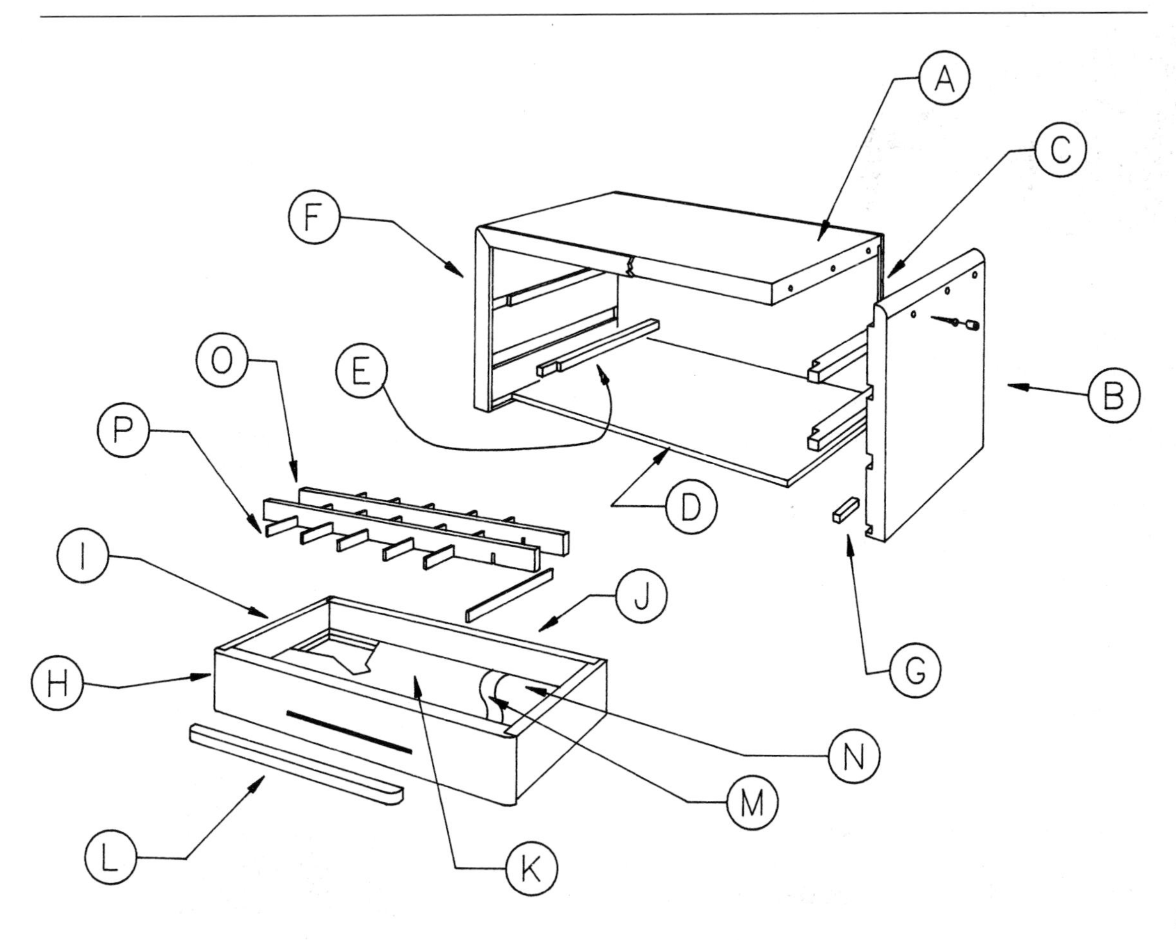

The Unseen Hinge

A Jewelry Box by Tony Lydgate

This straightforward design is ideal for jewelry, collectibles or other treasures. Clean lines and the striking contrast between highly-figured woods combine to create a beautiful visual statement.

WOODS

In the examples shown, the carcass and the center medallion of the lid are reversed combinations of Hawaiian koa and figured maple. Since it is a fairly small piece, select something spectacular from the available woods for the lid medallion.

MILLING

Follow the procedures for accurate miters outlined in the General Instructions, page 12, to mill the carcass parts. Glue up the carcass, then mill the four mitered lid border parts so that the finished lid will make a slightly oversize fit. The excess will be sanded off later. This design utilizes a floating panel or medallion in the center of the lid. A shallow rabbet around the perimeter of the lid on both faces produces a keel which fits into saw kerf dadoes in the lid border parts. For the most pleasing visual effect, the gap around the medallion should be a uniform 1/16".

The horizontal splines in the corners of the carcass, called "slipfeathers", are saw kerfs into which triangular pieces of contrasting wood are glued. Slipfeathers reinforce the glue joint and also add a graceful note to the design. See the General Instructions, page 12, for details on making slipfeathers.

ASSEMBLY

The lid is hinged to the carcass with a simple metal pin. Fabricate the carcass and the lid separately. Sand the edges of the lid on the 6" x 48" belt sander so that it fits inside the carcass with a gap of about 1/16" on the front and sides and slightly more on the rear. The rear gap is larger to allow for clearance when the lid opens. Center the lid in its proper position in the box carcass and use small folded strips of newspaper to jam it tight. Mark the hinge pin locations on the sides with an awl and use a drill press to drill the pin holes through the sides and into the lid edge.

A steel or brass pin of the appropriate diameter, or even a four-penny nail with the head nipped off, provides the hinge. Drive it in far enough to make room for a dowel plug made of the same wood as the carcass side.

The tray is designed to slide on rails. Its size and number of compartments may vary to suit its intended use.

SARAH
MICHAELS
SARAH
MICHAELS
ROSE MIST
body soap
SARAH
MICHAELS
SARAH
MICHAELS
SARAH
MICHAELS
SARAH
MICHAELS

MATERIALS: The Unseen Hinge, A Jewelry Box

Part	Description	Dimensions	Quantity
A	Front/back	5/8" x 3¼" x 12"	2
B	End	5/8" x 3¼" x 7½"	2
C	Bottom	1/8" x 6⅝" x 11⅛"	1
D	Bottom cardboard	6¼" x 10¾"	1
E	Bottom liner - velvet	7¼" x 11¾"	1
F	Box slipfeather	3/32" x 1" x 1"*	8
G	Tray rail	1/8" x 1/2" x 10¾"	2
H	Lid stop	1/8" x 3/8" x 10¾"	1
I	Lid front/back	1/2" x 1" x 10¾"	2
J	Lid end	1/2" x 1"x 6¼"	2
K	Lid medallion	1/2" x 4¾" x 9¼"	1
L	Lid slipfeather	3/32" x 1" x 1"*	4
M	Tray front/back	3/8" x 3/4" x 4¾"	2
N	Tray side	3/8" x 3/4" x 6"	2
O	Tray bottom	1/8" x 4¼" x 5½"	1
P	Tray cardboard	4" x 5¼"	1
Q	Tray liner - velvet	5" x 6¼"	1
R	Short divider	1/8" x 1/4" x 4¼"	2
S	Long divider	1/8" x 1/4" x 5½"	1
T	Pin	1/16" D. x 1" L.	2

**Final size*

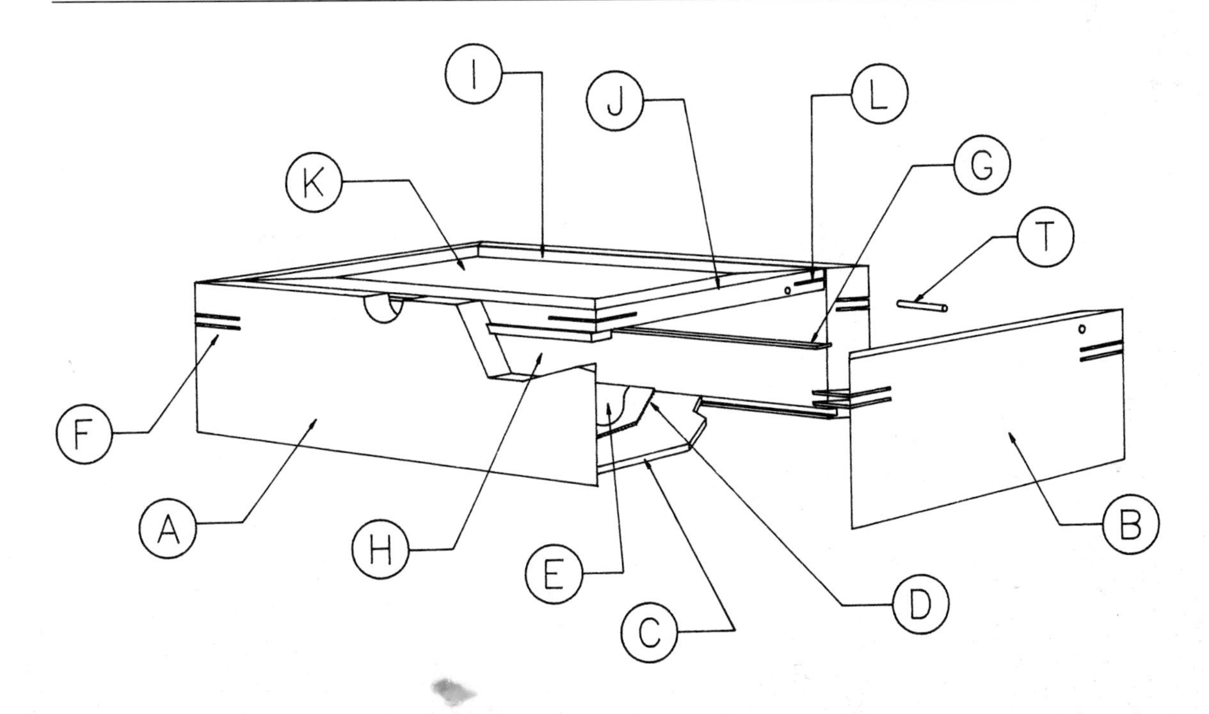

ORK
ES
BOOK
& Row

Lines of Grace

A Multi-purpose Box by Tony Lydgate

This simple but rich design provides the opportunity to use small pieces of contrasting woods. The box asks to be handled and opened. Though made to hold pens or pencils, it is also equally suited for jewelry or other keepsakes. Its delightfully sculptural form could decorate a coffee table, bedroom dresser or office.

WOODS

The examples shown are combinations of rosewood, bocote, koa, and maple, with contrasting slipfeathers and lid strips of these woods plus Indian rosewood and sateen or vermilion. Once the milling setups are complete, cutting the parts for this box takes only a moment. So plan on making a batch of four or more, each in a different combination of woods.

MILLING

Mill the miters on the carcass sides with the saw blade upright and the miter fence at a 45° angle. For the short sides, which are only 2" wide, use a spring clamp to hold the stock as it passes through the saw blade. Use masking tape to clamp while gluing. A solid wood bottom may be substituted, either dadoed into a saw kerf as shown, or glued into a rabbet to produce a flush bottom. The number and depth of slipfeathers may be varied to produce a more intricate effect. See the General Instructions, page 12 for details on slipfeathers.

MATERIALS: Lines of Grace, A Multi-purpose Box

Part	Description	Dimensions	Quantity
A	Side	5/16" x 1⅞" x 10"	2
B	End	5/16" x 1⅞" x 2"	2
C	Bottom	1/8" x 1¾" x 9¾"	1
D	Top	1/2" x 2" x 10"*	1
E	Slipfeather	3/32" x 3/8" x 1"	8

**Note that the top is laminated from contrasting woods, then cut to the final size.*

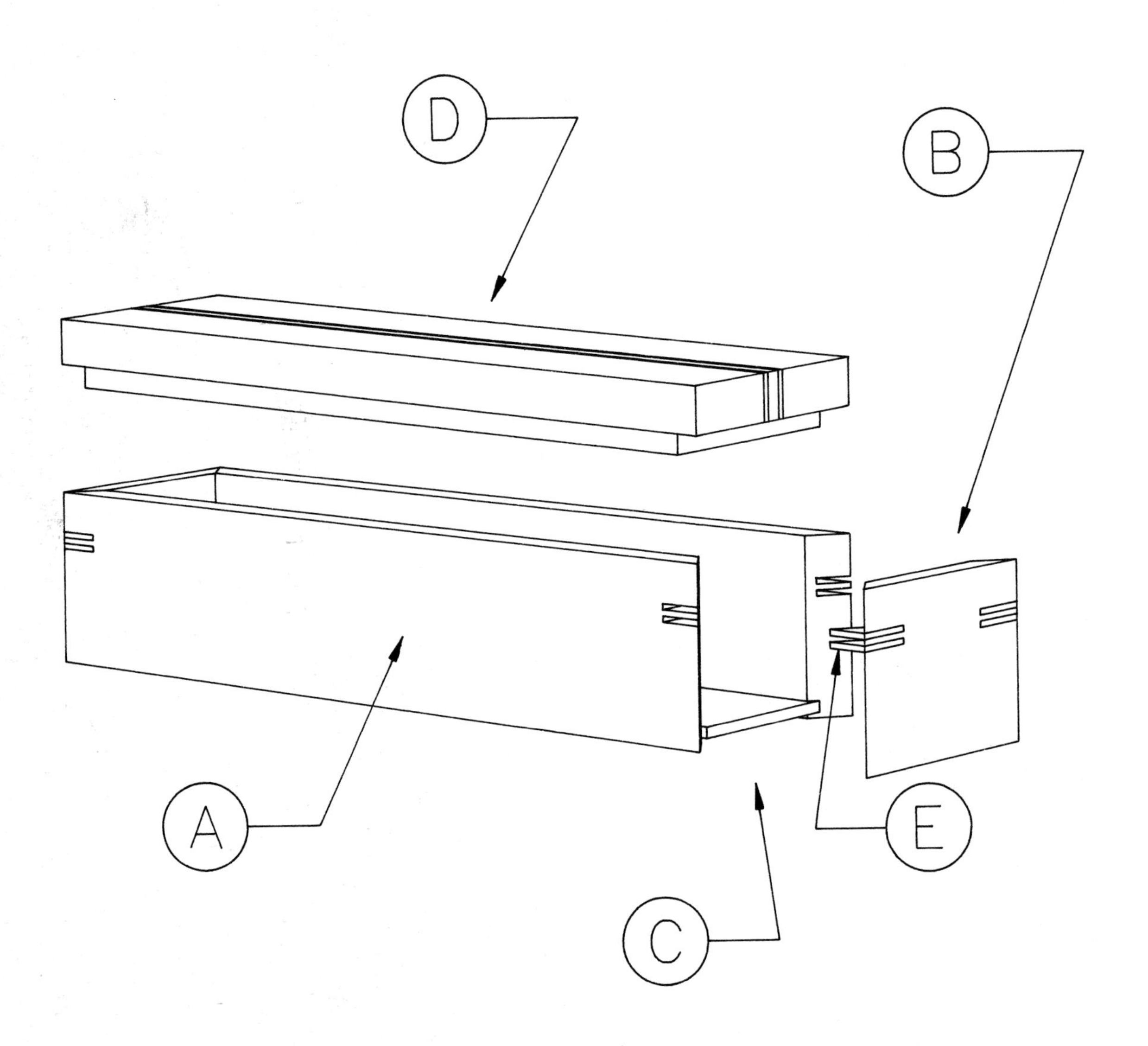

Ear of the Dog

A Box by Tony Lydgate

Careful attention to detail in the fabrication of this design results in a pleasingly intricate form. This box will be puzzled over, and once understood, marvelled over endlessly.

WOODS

The three examples in the photograph are Mexican bocote with maple "ears" and lid trim, Hawaiian koa with cocobolo "ears" and trim, and birdseye maple with bocote "ears" and trim. As with any diminutive box design, the dog-eared box offers an opportunity to utilize small pieces of interesting woods. The possible wood combinations are infinite.

MILLING

The carcass begins as a simple square box, 4⅜" on each side, 2¼" high, with mitered corners (see General Instructions, page 12) and a 1/8" plywood bottom glued into a saw kerf dado. As it takes little time to mill additional parts once the machine setups are complete, consider making this box in batches of four or more, using contrasting woods.

Use masking tape to clamp the glue joints; when dry, remove the tape and rough-cut off the corners of the box on a band saw. Set the band saw table at a 45° angle. Use a band saw miter fence, also set at 45°, to trim the corners of the box about 1/16" longer than their final dimension. Then move to the table saw and create the same double 45° setup to trim the box corners cleanly so that the "ears" can be glued on. Use the same band saw setup to mill the box lid. Since it will be sanded to its final size, the lid does not require an additional table saw cut.

ASSEMBLY

After the glued-on ears have dried, sand the carcass on the 6" x 48" sander to flush and smooth the four sides and the top. The lid liner, milled to just fit in the top opening, is chamfered, then glued to the underside of the rough-shaped lid. Apply glue to the liner, center the lid and liner on the box carcass and wait a few minutes for the glue to take. Then remove the whole assembly from the carcass. Clamp the liner tightly to the lid with two spring clamps. If the liner is clamped while the glue is still wet, it will "skate" around

To finish-shape the box, use masking tape across the middle of the four sides to hold the lid to the carcass. This keeps the lid in position for shaping the ears and the 45° bevel of the top to flush, using a 6"x 48" belt sander. Once the ears are shaped, remove all the masking tape and use fresh tape to secure the lid to the box over the ears. This will allow the same shaping operation to be performed on the four sides.

MATERIALS: Ear of the Dog, A Box

Part	Description	Dimensions	Quantity
A	Side	5/16" x 2¼" x 4⅜"	4
B	Bottom	1/8" x 4⅛" x 4⅛"	1
C	Ear	1/8" x 1¾" x 1¾"	4
D	Lid	1/2" x 4⅛" x 4⅛"	1
E	Lid border strip	1/8" x 1/2" x 3½"	4
F	Lid liner	1/4" x 3¾" x 3¾"	1

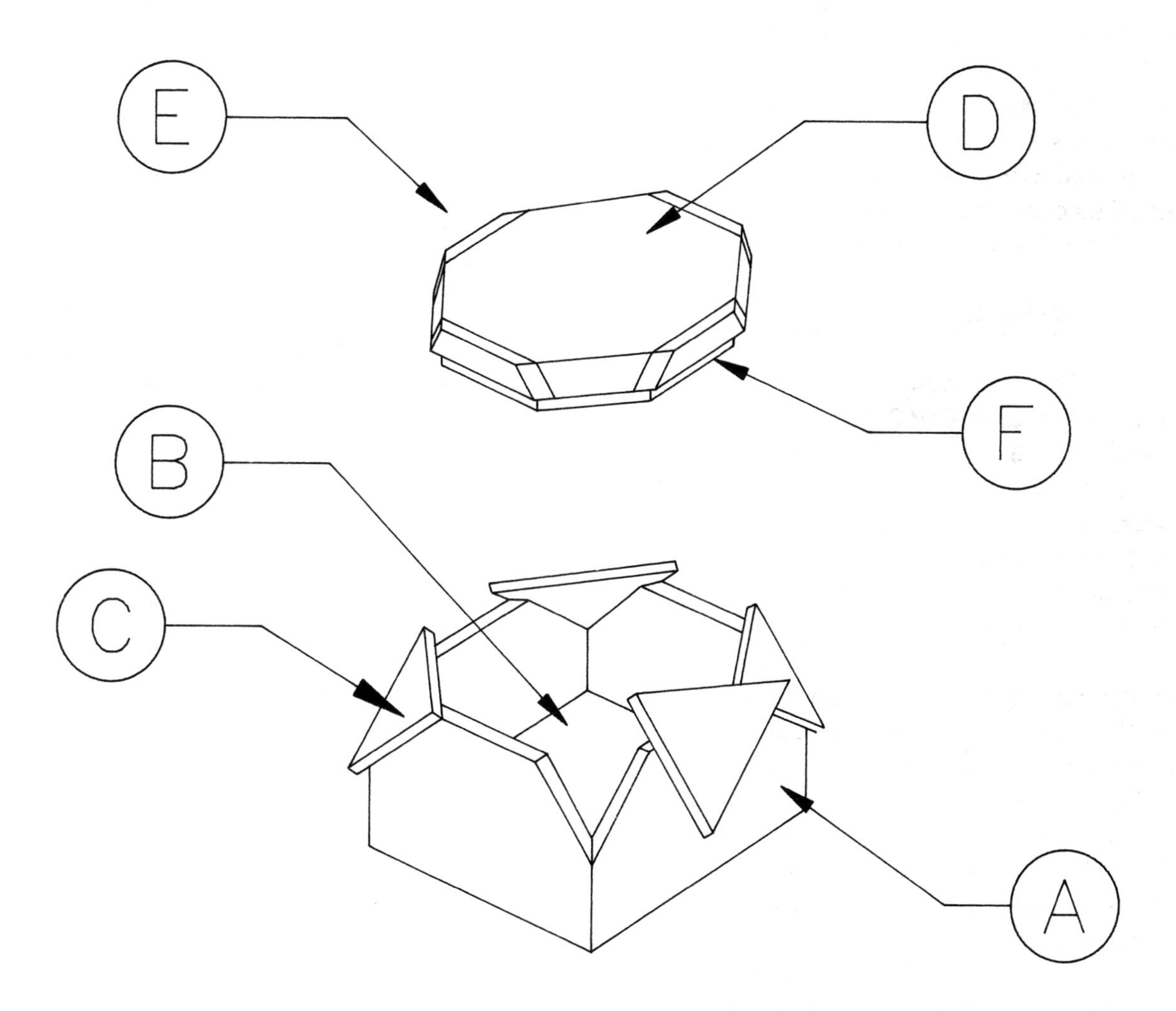

MORTON
FREE RUNNING
SALT

For Finery

A Bevel-side Jewelry Chest by Tony Lydgate

This design takes its shape from angled bevels cut on the table saw after the carcass has been glued up. The lid, formed from a central medallion surrounded by a laminated border, operates on an invisible pin hinge. The lid is also bevelled on the table saw. Its bevels are later sanded into curves, thus the subtle domed shape. The example shown is intended for jewelry, but this design can be easily adapted to numerous functions.

WOODS

The chest is shown in highly-figured Hawaiian koa. The contrasting dark wood used for slipfeathers and laminate strips is East Indian rosewood. Depending upon the degree of contrast desired, any combination of woods may be used, although the design benefits from the use of a dramatically figured medallion.

MILLING

Follow the standard procedures for milling a rectangular mitered-corner box. Glue up the carcass and lid, then slipfeather both. Let dry; sand all faces smooth. Drill the holes for the pin hinges through the sides and into the edges of the lid . Then angle the table saw blade to 16° and move the fence to the left side of the blade.

Pass the carcass between the fence and blade to cut the lower bevels on all four sides, then flip the box over and repeat for the upper bevels.

The laminate border around the lid medallion may be composed of strips of any preferred thickness. Mill the center medallion at least 7/8" thick to allow the eventual dome to be as high as possible. Bevel the lid at an 8° angle, with the fence once again to the left of the tablesaw blade. The resulting lid should be about 1/2" thick at the edges, with the hinge pin hole exactly centered vertically in the middle of the slipfeather.

ASSEMBLY

The laminate strips forming the lid border are glued up ahead of time and later mitered to fit around the medallion like a frame around a picture. Using 3/4" plywood, make a jig for gluing the laminates: one piece 21" x 6" to act as a "plate" to keep everything flat; two pieces each 21" x 2" to protect the outside edges of the laminate rods from clamp marks and equalize clamp pressure; and two smaller pieces, placed on top of the rods and clamped to the plate, one on each end sandwich-style, to prevent the entire assembly from buckling.

For convenience, the laminates are made in a 21" length that will yield one long and one short side when crosscut prior to mitering. Hence two rods are required for one chest lid.

Glue them up using at least three transverse clamps, and use two short clamps, one at each end vertically, to provide the needed sandwich squeeze. Line the plywood plate and the sandwich blocks with newspaper to prevent the work from gluing itself to the gluing jig.

After the carcass and lid have been completely fabricated, slipfeathered and pinned and their bevels cut on the table saw, the 6" x 48" sander will perfect and polish the angled faces.

The process is not unlike faceting a gemstone: use a sharp 150x grit belt to sand the facets smooth, then a finer or "polishing" belt to produce a glass-like surface. Scraping, vibrating, or hand sanding are also possible, depending on the hardness of the wood, but be careful to keep the facets and bevelled angles of the carcass crisp-looking. Rock the lid back and forth on the sander to blend the straight angles of the table saw bevels into rounded curves. Then perfect and polish the dome shape with a vibrator. Tray, tray dividers, and velvet pads may be added (see the General Instructions).

MATERIALS: For Finery, A Bevel-side Jewelry Chest

Part	Description	Dimensions	Quantity
A	Front/back	13/16" x 4" x 14"	2
B	Side	13/16" x 4" x 9"	2
C	Bottom	1/8" x 8" x 13"	1
D	Bottom cardboard	7⅜" x 12⅜"	1
E	Carcass slipfeather	3/32" x 1⅛" x 2"	12
F	Lid slipfeather	3/32" x 1⅛" x 2"	4
G	Lid medallion	7/8" x 5⅜" x 10⅜"	1
H	Lid border lam strip	1/8" x 13/16" x 21"	8
I	Lid border lam strip	3/32" x 13/16" x 21"	4
J	Lid border lam strip	13/16" x 1/2" x 21"	2
K	Tray support rail	1/8" x 5/8" x 7⅜"	2
L	Lid support post	5/16" x 5/16" x 1½"	2
M	Hinge pin	1/8" D. x 1" L.	2
N	Tray side	3/8" x 13/16" x 12¼"	2
O	Tray side	3/8" x 13/16" x 5"	2
P	Tray bottom	1/8" x 4⅝" x 11⅞"	1
Q	Tray cardboard	4¾" x 11½"	1
R	Tray divider	3/8" x 1/2" x 11½"	1
S	Tray divider	1/8" x 5/16" x 4¾"	4

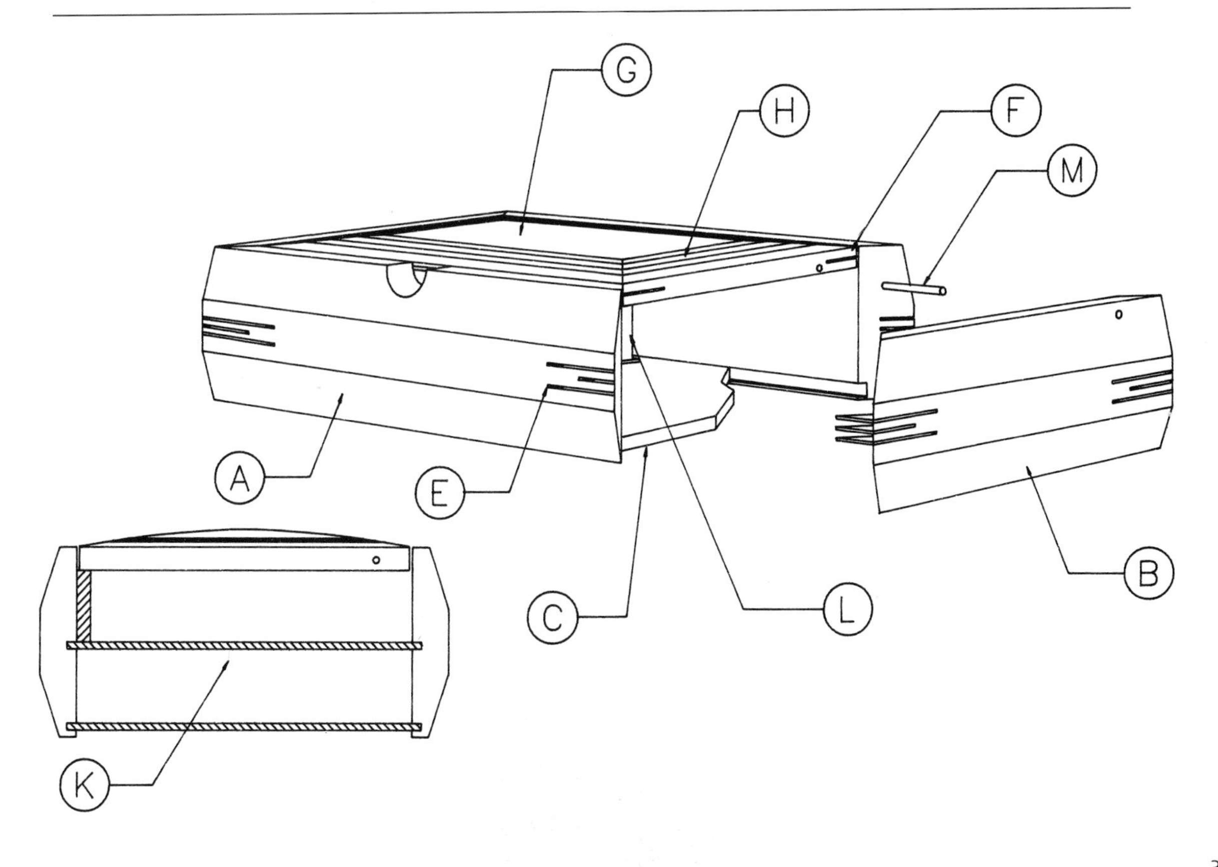

LESS THAN 1 CALORIE
SPICE
tea

Tea Celebration

A Tea Keeper by John Foster

This elegant box by John Foster is an essential accessory for anyone who enjoys brewing tea. The six lidded compartments are designed to hold an assortment of loose teas or teabags, along with a tea infuser.

WOODS

Foster has selected a rich, dark piece of California walnut for this box. The six handles of the compartment lids are each of a different wood, adding color to the design and helping to identify each compartment's contents. Indian rosewood, sateen, bocote, cocobolo, quilted maple and pernambuco were used, but any contrasting woods will serve equally well.

MILLING

The carcass is a straightforward mitered design, with veneer plywood bottom and top inserted into pre-cut dadoes. The carcass is ripped in two after gluing. Mortices for the hinges are hand-chiselled.

The interior compartment dividers are notched for easy assembly and a snug fit. Using a dado blade, the undersides of the lids are rabbeted on the table saw allowing them to sit tightly in their compartments. The recesses into which the handles are set are drilled with a Forstner or similar flat-bottomed drill bit and a rail is attached to the rear of the box to provide a stop for the opened lid.

ASSEMBLY

Prior to gluing up the carcass, the entire interior of the box and the veneer faces are polish-sanded, and the top rim is sanded and rounded slightly where the top veneer plywood fits into its dado. Compartment dividers are trimmed to fit, polish-sanded and glued in after the carcass has been ripped in two. Lids are fitted, handle holes and handles prepared, then glued in.

Finish Note: Because of the likelihood of contact with liquids, use a water resistant finish such as varnish.

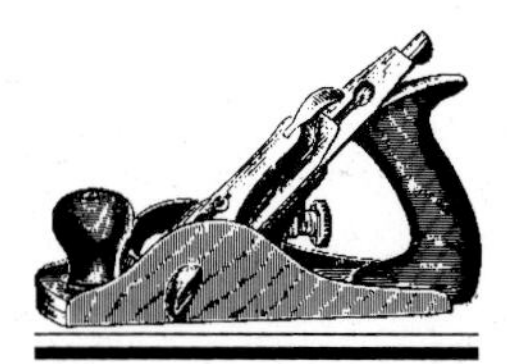

MATERIALS: Tea Celebration, A Tea-keeper

Part	Description	Dimensions	Quantity
A	Top	1/4" x 9¾" x 15¼"	1
B	Bottom	1/8" x 9¾" x 15¼"	1
C	Front/back	5/8" x 3" x 16"	2
D	Side	5/8" x 3" x 10½"	2
E	Rear lid support	1/2" x 2" x 12"	1
F	Compartment divider-short	3/8" x 2" x 9¼"	2
G	Compartment divider-long	3/8" x 2" x 14¼"	3
H	Compartment divider-short	3/8" x 2" x 8½"	2
I	Compartment lid	1/2" x 4½" x 4½"	6
J	Lid handle	5/16" x 5/8" x 1½"	6
K	Brass hinge	1¼" x 1½"	2

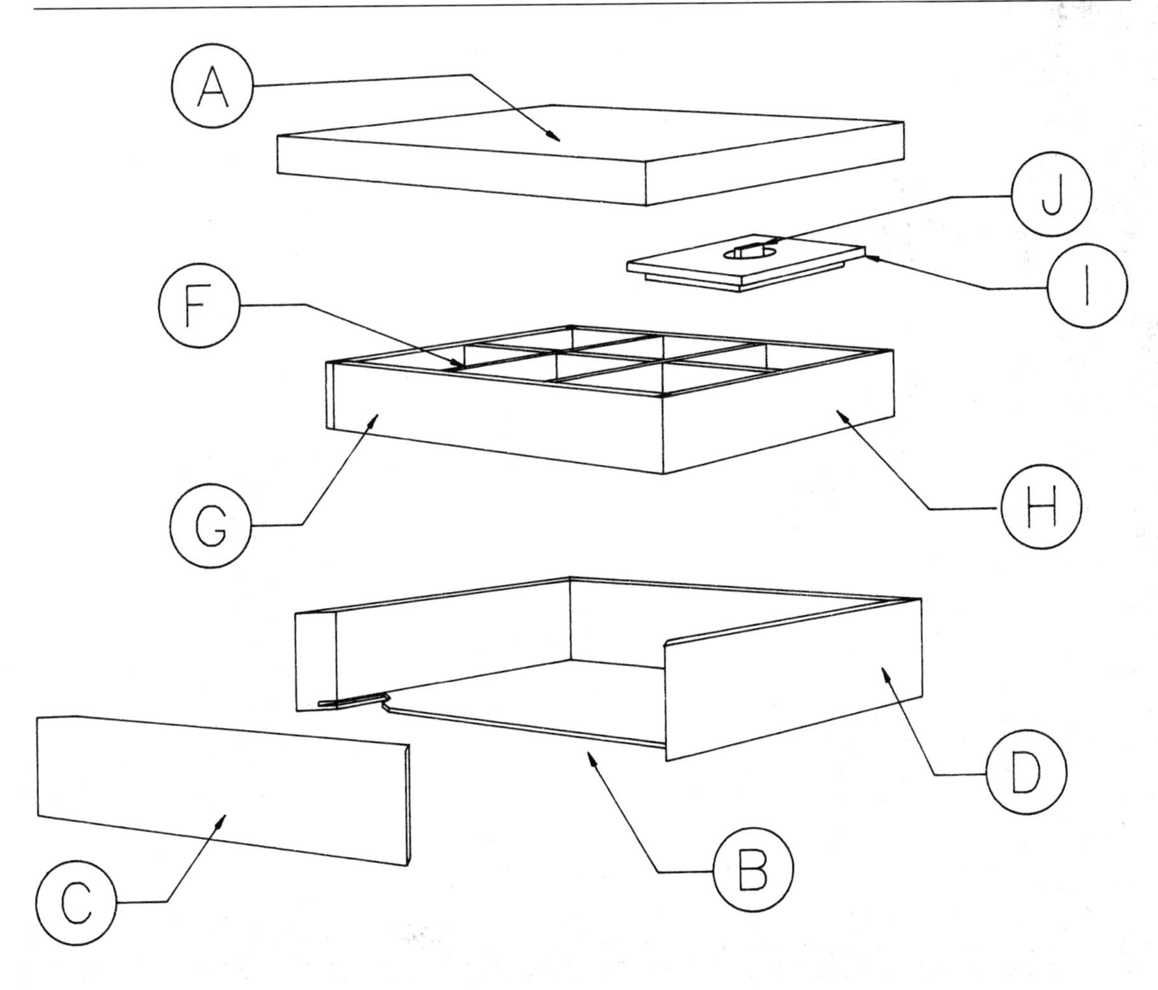

Eight Delights

A Jewelry Chest by Tony Lydgate

This chest uses double-miter, frame-and-panel construction to showcase seven velvet-lined horizontal drawers. The eighth delight, a unique vertical drawer for earring and necklace storage, provides graceful balance to the design.

WOODS

The chest shown is western quilted and curly maple with contrasting handles of East Indian rosewood. Oak, ash, eastern maple, birch or cherry, or darker woods like koa, mahogany or walnut may also be used.

MILLING

To prepare the stock for the frame, start with 5/4" (1¼") or thicker material. Rip and finish-sand to dimension, preferably using a thickness sander for accuracy. With the idea of creating the most harmonious presentation of grain, lay out the stock as it will appear in the finished chest. Label all pieces, showing which face is at the front. Mil' the saw kerf slots and the 1/4" dado for the back, then the double 45° miters with the miter fence on the table saw. These must be accurate, so experiment with some trial stock to be sure the cutting setup is entirely satisfactory.

The solid wood panels on the top and sides are glued to the 1/8" plywood liner. These panels are milled slightly on the narrow side to allow the wood to expand. But wood can also shrink, exposing more of the underlying plywood than desired, so do not make them too scant in width. The 45° bevels around the panel edges are cut on the table saw with the blade angled, then finish-sanded on the 6" x 48" sander and polished by hand or vibrator sander. The drawers employ simple rabbet joint construction. Substitute finger joints, dovetails, or slipfeathers for a more elaborate effect.

The slotted earring racks should be as thin as practical to accommodate post-style earrings. The shallow notches are simply saw kerfs. Consider using rosewood or a similar dense and strong hardwood for these parts.

The drawer handles have a keel which fits into a saw kerf milled into the drawer fronts. This simplifies centering and also produces a stronger assembly.

ASSEMBLY

Make sure all the double-mitered frame parts are carefully polished with the edges slightly softened. First, assemble the parts dry, without glue, to be sure everything fits and rehearse the steps. Fine-sand the veneer face of the 1/4" thick back panel, then glue up the back and its enclosing frame, using tape to clamp the joints and a square to ensure right angles. Glue up the front frame assembly at the same time.

After half an hour, use a sharp chisel to remove any excess glue accumulated in the double miter joint valleys. Then glue the whole box together by connecting the front frame and back frame assemblies with the four 10" connecting frames parts, placing the 1/8" top and side plywood sheets in between. Check for squareness again, then bring the chisel back in a little while to remove the errant glue.

Make the chest base and glue it into the carcass, positioning the top of the base exactly flush with the tops of the lower frame members so the bottom drawer and vertical earring drawer will slide smoothly.

The drawers ride on 1/4" plywood platforms, faced with strips of the same hardwood as the drawer fronts. These platforms are dadoed into two pieces of 1/2" plywood, also faced.

This assembly should be prepared separately, then glued into the frame-and-panel carcass. Finally, glue on the side and top panels. Drawers may be lined with velvet, and dividers tailored to fit the treasures they will receive.

MATERIALS: Eight Delights, A Jewelry Chest

Part	Description	Dimensions	Quantity
A	Vertical frame member	1⅛" x 1⅛" x 18"	4
B	Horizontal frame member	1⅛" x 1⅛" x 14"	4
C	Connecting frame member	1⅛" x 1⅛" x 10"	4
D	Back	1/4" x 13" x 17"	1
E	Side liner	1/8" x 9" x 17"	2
F	Top liner	1/8" x 9" x 13"	1
G	Side panel	3/4" x 7¾" x 15¾"	2
H	Top panel	3/4" x 11¾" x 11¾"	1
I	Base frame	3/8" x 1½" x 11¾"	2
J	Base frame	3/8" x 1½" x 7¾"	2
K	Base top	1/4" x 7½" x 11½"	1
L	Drawer cage side	1/2" x 8⅝" x 15¾"	2
M	Drawer cage facing	1/8" x 1/2" x 15¾"	2
N	Drawer platforms	1/4" x 8" x 8⅝"	6
O	Drawer platform facing	1/8" x 1/4" x 7½"	6
P	Vertical drawer front/back	3/4" x 3¾" x 15¾"	2
Q	Vertical drawer top/bottom	3/4" x 3¾" x 8"	2
R	Earring rack	1/8" x 5/8"x 7½"	12
S	Earring rack support	1/4" x 3/4" x 14¼"	2
T	Vertical drawer handle	3/8" x 5/8" x 7½"	1
U	Drawer front	3/8" x 2¼" x 7½"	7
V	Drawer back	3/8" x 2¼" x 7¼"	7
W	Drawer side	3/8" x 2¼" x 8½"	14
X	Drawer bottom	1/8" x 7⅛" x 8¼"	7
Y	Drawer handle	3/8" x 5/8" x 4¼"	7

The diagram for this box is on page 48.

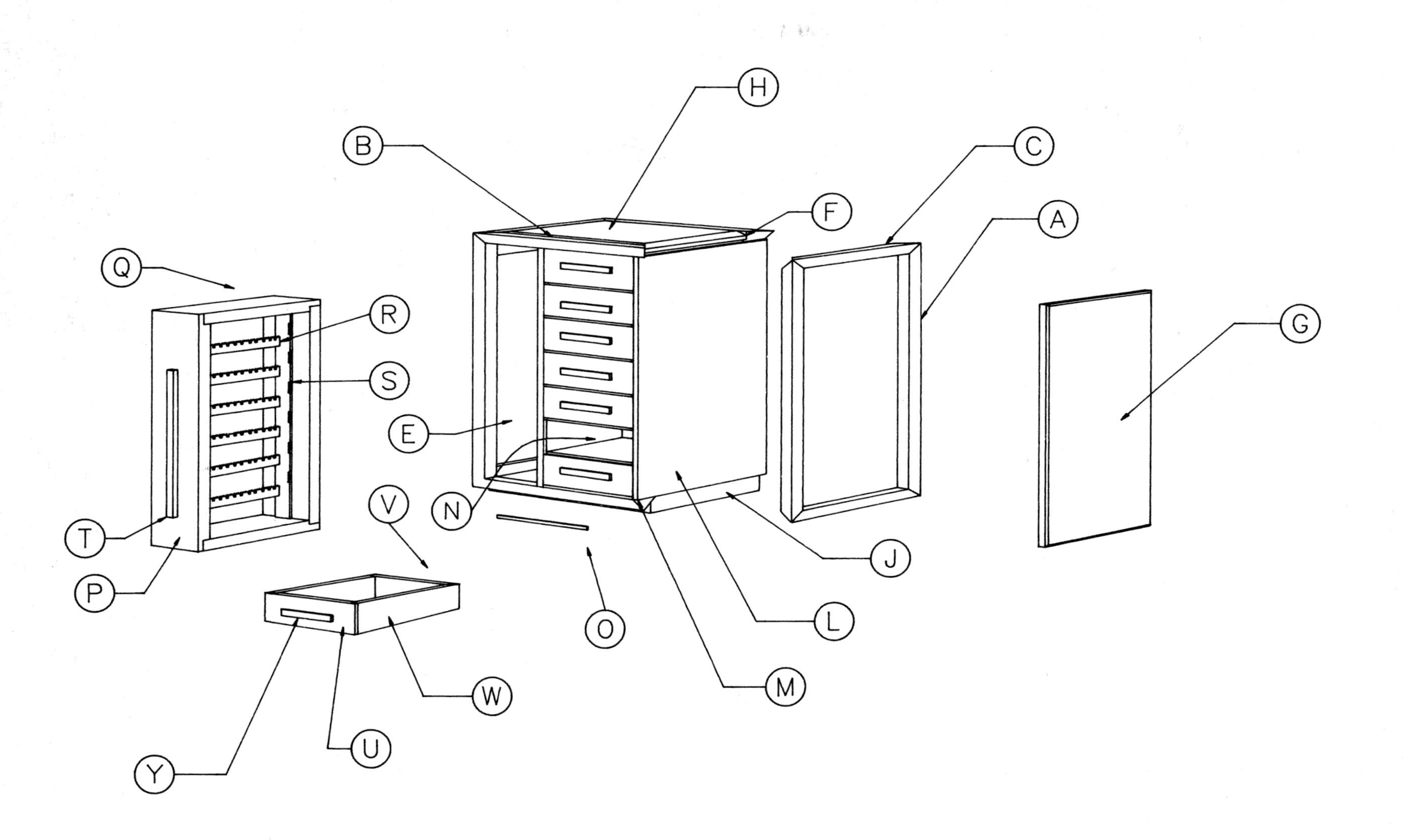
H
B
F
C
A
G
Q
R
S
E
V
N
T
P
J
O
L
M
W
Y
U

Tibles Dibles House

A Dual-purpose Box by Tony Lydgate

This whimsical box with its suggestion of a sheltering roof may be designed to house either collec**tibles** or e**dibles.** It is also equipped with a handle for easy carrying.

WOODS

The collectibles version is California walnut, with the tray rails and roof elements of pernambuco. The smaller version is perfect for edibles such as hors d'oeuvres or snacks. It is of Hawaiian koa and Indian rosewood. This design especially welcomes experimentation with interesting woods and wood combinations.

MILLING

The basic structure consists of two post-and-beam assemblies, reinforced with a solid bottom and back. These are tied together with thin rails doubling as tray supports. Use a table saw to mill the dadoes in the underside of the horizontal top beams and the dadoes that will receive the back and bottom.

The table saw blade will mill the kerfs in the upright posts which receive the tray support rails. Finish-sand the posts, beams and back, and glue up the front and rear assemblies, using a square to ensure right angles. Allow both assemblies to dry thoroughly. Set the table saw miter fence to 15° and create a stop block system that will allow the milling of saw kerf slots across the tops of the post-and-beams.

Make the top central roof beam and tray support rails. Glue the edging to the front and sides of the bottom; trim and sand it to size. The tray support rails, like all the parts of this project, must be both finish-sanded and precisely dimensioned prior to gluing. Each piece should make a clean but tight fit. To be sure the parts fit, assemble all dry, except the eight 1/8" strips that make up the roof element. Then glue up, omitting the roof strips.

After approximately half an hour, when the glue has set but not completely hardened, return with a sharp chisel and carefully remove all excess glue. Finally, sand and polish the roof strips, miter their ends, and glue them in.

Trays are fabricated using the standard tray technique in the General Instructions, page 13. Use an oil finish if the trays will be lined with velvet; if the box is intended for food presentation, use a water-resistant finish such as varnish.

MATERIALS: Tibles Dibles House, A Dual-purpose Box

Part	Description	Dimensions	Quantity
A	Upright post	3/4" x 3/4" x 11¼"	4
B	Horizontal crossbeam	3/4" x 3/4" x 14½"	2
C	Roof beam/handle	13/16" x 1" x 8⅜"	1
D	Back	1/4" x 11⅜" x 11¾"	1
E	Bottom	1/8" x 6⅞" x 12½"	1
F	Roof strip	1/8" x 3/4" x 9⅛"	8
G	Bottom edging	1/8" x 1/8" x 7"	2
H	Bottom facing	1/8" x 1/4" x 12¾"	1
I	Tray side	5/16" x 13/16" x 11⅛"	10
J	Tray side	5/16" x 13/16" x 6⅝"	10
K	Tray bottom	1/8" x 6⅝" x 10¾"	5
L	Tray stopblock	1/4" x 3/8" x 3/4"	10
M	Tray rail	1/8" x 1⅛" x 7"	8

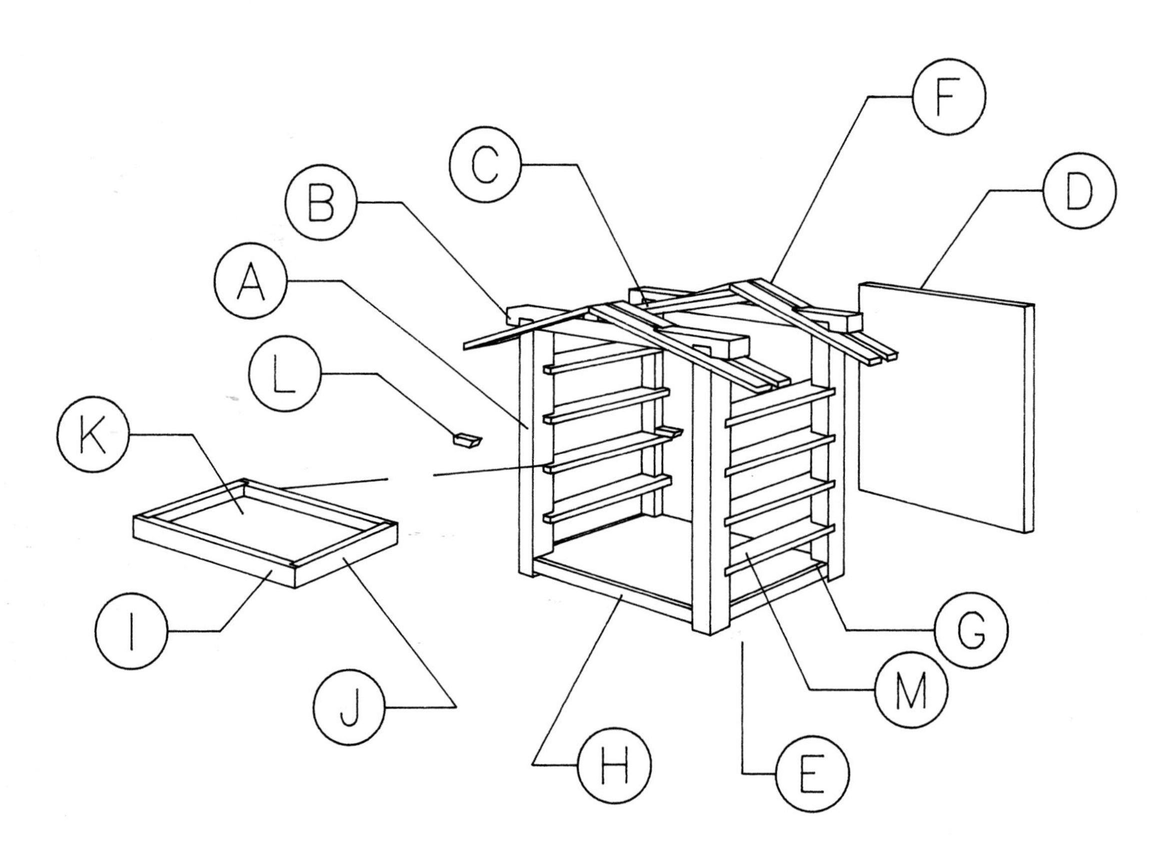

Mountain Stronghold

A Box with Visible Drawer Tracks by Tony Lydgate

This fascinating box makes its drawer tracks visible rather than concealing them inside the carcass, thus they become an important design element. This version has two pairs of drawers set at right angles to each other and running the entire 14" length of the piece. The basic idea behind this box invites many variations, including addition of more levels of drawers and reduction or enlargement in scale.

WOODS

Birdseye maple and dark East Indian rosewood were selected for their stark black and white contrast, but any combination of light and dark woods may be used.

MILLING

Dimension and fine-sand the eight legs as uniformly as possible. Stand the legs on end in their approximate final position on the work table, arranging them to present the most attractive grain pattern, then label each. A series of 3/8" wide dadoes are cut 1/4" deep into each leg to receive the edges of the top panels and the rails on which the drawers slide. The locations of these dadoes vary, so study the plan to determine how the design is put together. Milling a set of test pieces first is also helpful.

The two rectangular panels forming the top of the box have edges detailed with the table saw. The sharper the blade, the less scraping and/or sanding these detail cuts will require prior to finishing. Edge facings are glued to both ends of these parts before assembly. The exact width and length of these ultimately determines the final dimensions of the box. The drawers are milled and assembled after the carcass has been glued up. If they are made slightly long, they can then be sanded to a flush fit with the box sides. Mill the dado slots on the outsides of the drawer bodies using a dado blade or router; with either tool, avoid chip-out at the end of the cut.

These slots should be slightly wider and deeper than the rails they will run on to allow for ease of drawer movement. A gap of about 1/16" should be left around the top and also on either side of the drawer to prevent sticking or binding.

ASSEMBLY

To assemble the carcass, first prepare four scrap plywood pieces of any thickness to fit between the legs at their base. These will hold the legs in place for straight and true assembly while gluing. Make sure the dimensions at the top and base of the box are the same after the rectangular top parts are fitted in. The task of assembling and gluing tops and rails is exacting; a dry assembly without glue is recommended.

About half an hour after gluing, remove excess glue on the rails or legs with a sharp chisel. Fine-sand and glue on the small trim pieces that serve as end caps on the drawer rails. Depending upon the amount of play in the drawers as they slide along their rails, the vertical front edges of the drawer fronts may need to be slightly rounded to prevent catching on the inside edges of the legs.

An oil finish will make the drawers slide smoothly. Use velvet pads for drawer lining and any system of drawer dividers suited to the intended use.

MATERIALS: Mountain Stronghold, A Box with Visible Drawer Tracks

Part	Description	Dimension	Quantity
A	Leg	7/8" x 7/8" x 11"	8
B	Drawer rail	1/2" x 3/8" x 14"	8
C	Top	3/4" x 6⅛" x 13¾"	2
D	Top edging	1/8" x 3/8" x 6⅛"	4
E	Drawer rail end cap	1/16" x 3/8" x 1/2"	16
F	Drawer side	3/8" x 2½" x 13"	8
G	Drawer front	3/4" x 2½" x 5½"	8
H	Drawer bottom	1/8" x 5⅛" x 13"	4

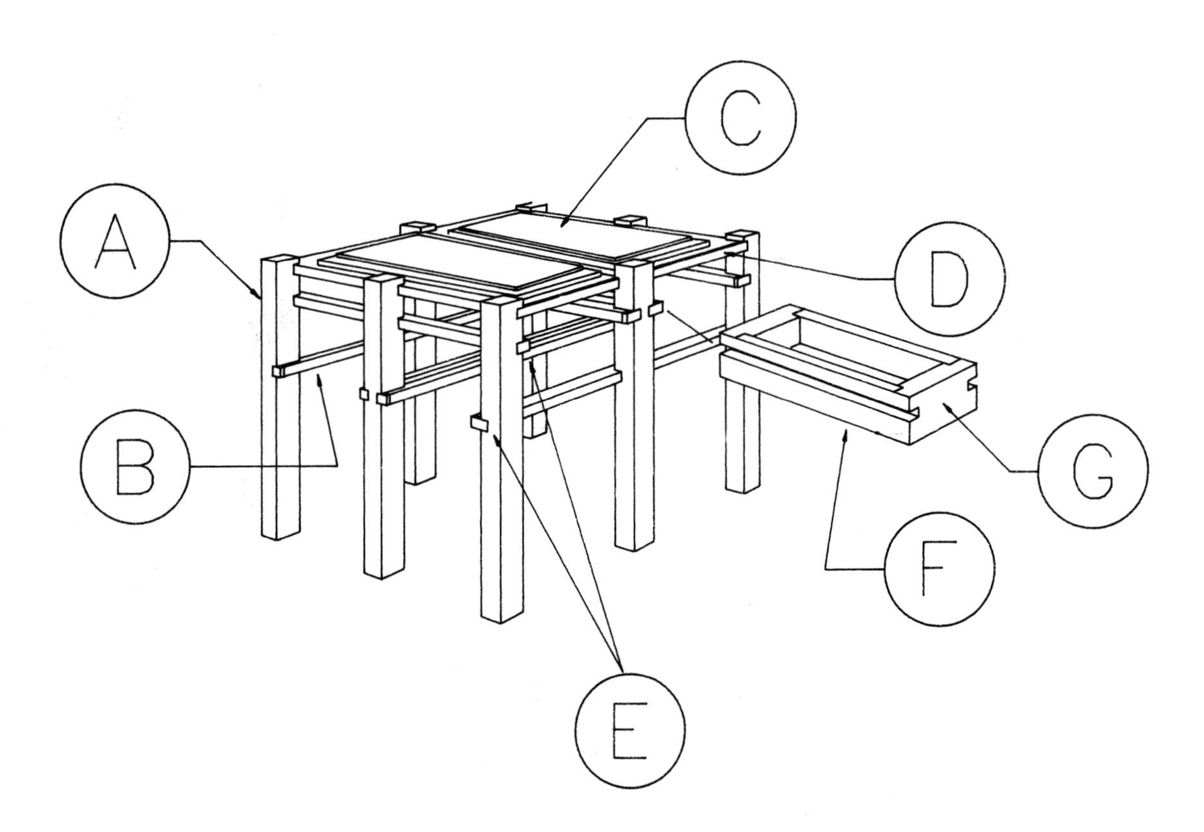

Touch and Turn

A Pivot-top Box by Anthony Beverly

This easy-to-make pivot-top box designed by Anthony Beverly uses domestic and exotic woods, both solids and veneers. The eye-catching design begs to be touched.

WOODS

The boxes shown contain ebony, cherry, padouk, walnut, mahogany, lacewood and madrone burl. Beverly deliberately selects a wide variety of combinations.

MILLING

The body of the box consists of two sides glued to end blocks of contrasting wood. The two ends are first crosscut from 2" thick stock, sanded on their inside faces, then glued to the 3/8" thick bottom. This assembly is then trimmed flush on the edges, and the two sides, which can be ripped from the same stock, are glued on. Sanding smoothes the carcass and rounds the edges. A 3/8"-diameter hole is drilled for the lid dowel.

The lid is 3/4" thick with an inset panel of veneer. Beautiful though the solid woods of the box are, Beverly saves the most spectacular figured veneers for this top panel. The lid edge rails are glued on, the contrasting pivot dowel is inserted and the lid is then sanded and polished like the rest of the box. Avoid sanding through the veneer on the lid.

MATERIALS: Touch and Turn, A Pivot-top Box

Part	Description	Dimensions	Quantity
A	Side	1/2" x 2¼" x 6"	2
B	Bottom	3/8" x 3⅛" x 6"	1
C	End	1" x 2" x 3⅛"	1
D	End	2" x 2" x 3⅛"	1
E	Lid body	3/4" x 3⅛" x 6"	1
F	Lid veneer inset	3⅛" x 3⅞"	1
G	Lid edge rail	1/2" x 3/4" x 6"	2
H	Pivot dowel	3/8" x 1½"	1

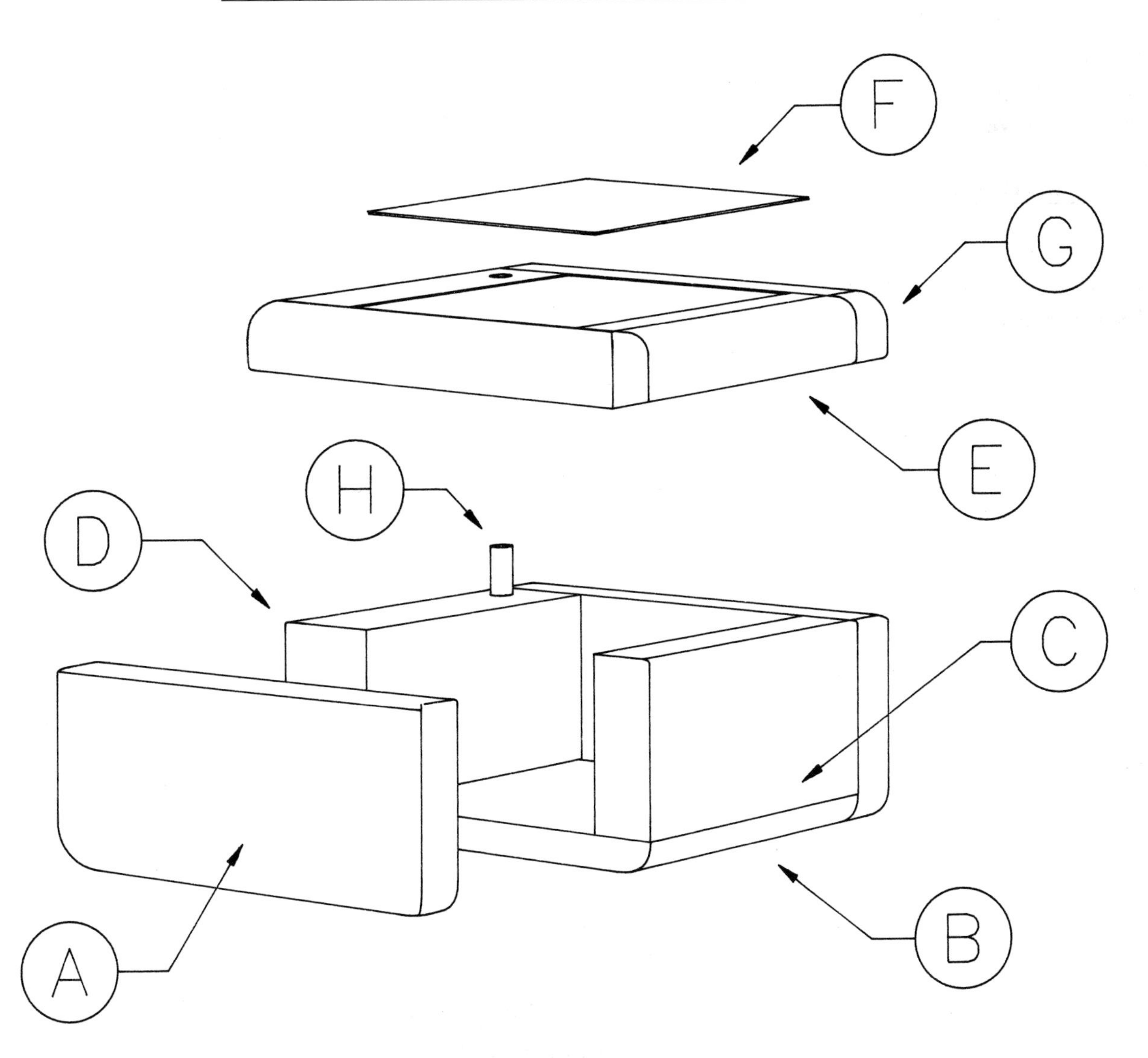

Simple Beauty

A Recipe Box by Brad Smith

This design is an ideal project for multiple fabrication. The tool set-ups for milling the finger joints take time, but once they are prepared, making several boxes at once is simple. Smith's technique for creating the lid produces eight at a time, cut from an 18"-diameter lathe-turned circle.

WOODS

The box shown is of walnut. Any hardwood, dark or light, is suitable.

MILLING

Finger joints can be milled on a table saw, using a dado blade, or with a router, using appropriate jigs. What appears to be an irregular curve on the lid is actually one of eight pieces cut from the 18" lathe-turned circle mentioned above. Four 13/16" x 4½" x 18" pieces are edge-glued, and the resulting plate is turned to produce raised ridges. These may be any shape desired. The finished turning is then ripped and crosscut into separate lids, following the pattern diagrammed.

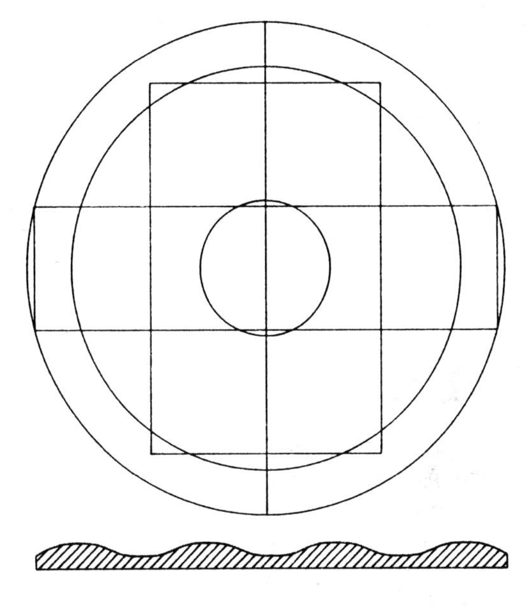

Profile of Turning

An undetectable seam can be produced on the bottom by covering the 1/4" plywood, its hardwood surface glued up facing inside, with a piece of thin walnut veneer.

MATERIALS: Simple Beauty, A Recipe Box

Part	Description	Dimensions	Quantity
A	Front/back	1/4" x 3⅝" x 5⅝"	2
B	Side	1/4"x 4" x 3¾" to 4⅛"	2
C	Top	3/4" x 4⅛" x 5"	1
D	Bottom	1/4" x 3⅝" x 5⅜"	1
E	Bottom veneer	4" x 5⅝"	1
F	Hinge pin	1/8" D. x 3/4" L.	2

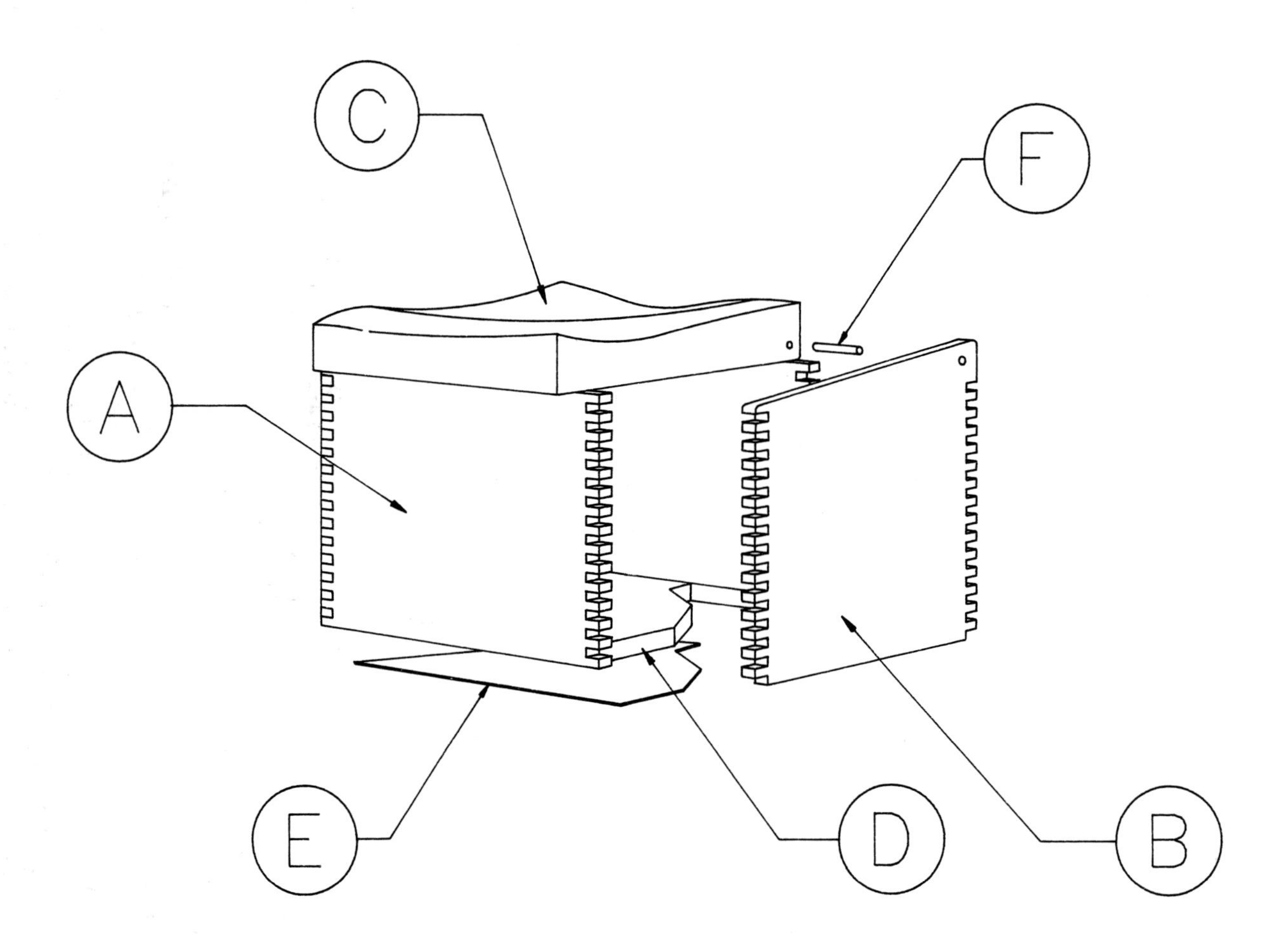

Freeform Spirit

A Hinged-lid Box by Charles Cobb

Sensuous curves and intriguing organic shapes disguise the simple construction of this inviting box by California designer Charles Cobb. Freeform designs invite variation and offer infinite opportunities to experiment with alternate shapes.

WOODS

The body and lid are Hawaiian koa and the contrasting dark wood of the handle is wenge. The more highly-figured the lumber, the more dramatic the effect of the piece.

MILLING

The carcass uses the most basic and simple joinery: the front and back are butted within the sides. Use stock at least 7/8" thick for the sides to permit later shaping and angling. Thicker stock allows more pronounced and dramatic irregular curves.

The front and back are milled lower than the sides so the lids can swing open. The 1/4" plywood for the bottom is dadoed into all four sides for added strength. Where the dadoes are visible in the front and back, Cobb has used 1/4" square filler plugs of wenge, matching the lid handle.

Lid stock should be at least 1¾" thick. Greater thickness offers more intriguing play with the hills and valleys that make the lid interesting. To fashion the lid, start with a block big enough to completely cover the carcass.

Rabbet the undersides of the butt edges across the grain so the lid will drop in and sit on the top edges of the sides. Allow 1/8" clearance between the lid and top edges of front and back. Band saw this block into four pieces, leaving an irregular gap between the two halves that varies from 1/4" to 3/8". The gap will be filled later by the contrasting handle.

ASSEMBLY

Glue up the carcass as a simple rectangle. To reinforce the butt joints, drill 1/8" diameter holes through the sides in either a symmetrical or irregular pattern. Then glue in contrasting wood dowels shaped by hand on the 6" x 48" sander. Using this same tool, rough-shape the lid parts. Polish them by hand or with a vibrator sander. Glue each pair together to form the halves of the top.

While shaping these irregular forms, preserve sufficient contact at their base for a secure glue joint. Sand and polish their sides and undersides, rounding the edges below the hinge pin so they will swing clear when opened. Jam them in position with folded bits of paper.

Drill holes for and install the hinge pins. If these are brass, the ends may be left visible. To hide them, sink them deeper and plug the holes with a small dowel.

This ugly duckling of a rough carcass, with its elegant swan of an oversize lid, is now ready to be sculpted into a unique and truly marvelous form.

Using the 6"x 48" sander or other sanding or shaping tools, modify the shape of the box, lid and all, until it matches the photograph, or until it pleases its creator.

Thoroughly polish the end grain of the lid. Shape and polish the handle; glue it on. Make sure the glue-side contour of the handle permits a secure joint, and leave sufficient room on the front-facing side for clearance when the lids are opened.

FINISHING

An oil finish will highlight the grain's changes of direction over the contours of the curves. Since sanding between coats of lacquer or varnish would be impractical in such inaccessible spaces, oil is the best finish for this box.

MATERIALS: Freeform Spirit, A Hinged-lid Box

Part	Description	Dimensions	Quantity
A	Front/back	3/4" x 3" x 5½"	2
B	Side	7/8" x 3½" x 6"	2
C	Bottom	1/4" x 5" x 6"	1
D	Top	1¾" x 6" x 7"	1
E	Handle	1" x 1¾" x 8½"	1
G	Hinge pin	5/32" D. x 1" L.	2
H	Filler block	1/4" x 1/4" x 1/2"	4

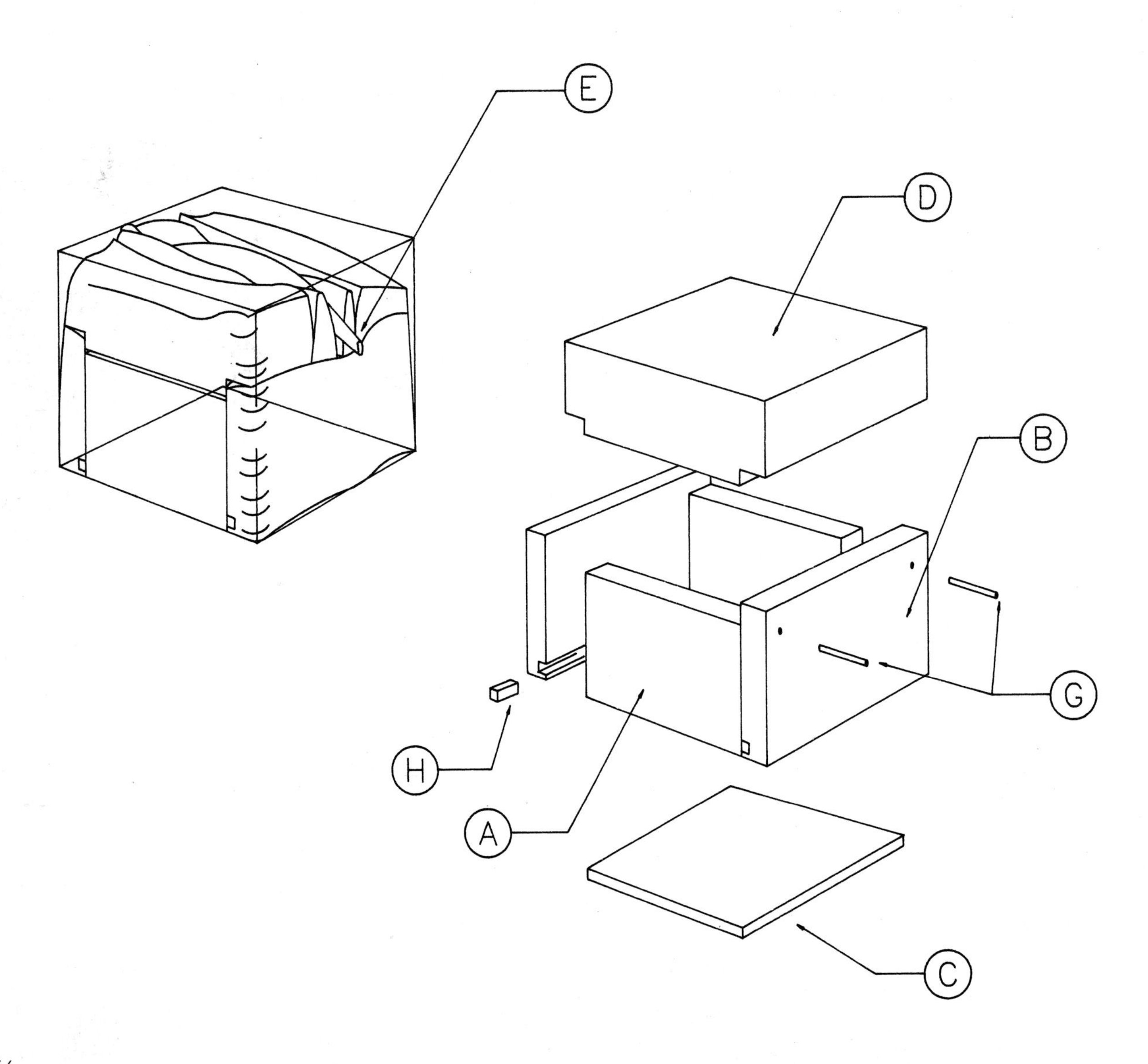

KEYS
OF THE
HEAR
THIS

Woodscape

A Marquetry Box by Gary Upton

Marquetry – the application of thin veneers in a decorative surface pattern – is among the most challenging of woodworking techniques. Success requires both technical skill and aesthetic sense. California designer Gary Upton demonstrates both in this box, creating a mountain landscape, then adding exquisite teardrop-shaped wooden hinges and an intricate hidden latch.

WOODS

Upton has selected a subtly-figured, golden Hawaiian koa for the body of this box; the thick, meaty stock ensures a generous roundover. The bottom and the surface onto which the top marquetry is glued are both 1/4" walnut veneer plywood. Traditional-style veneers, each about 1/28" thick, were used to

create the top design in koa, walnut, narra, and Brazilian and Indian rosewood. Cloth- and paper-backed veneers in a variety of species are also widely available. The wooden hinges are Indian rosewood, but any dense hardwood may be substituted. The latch dowel is osage orange, the inner dividers are aromatic Spanish cedar.

MILLING

The carcass is a straightforward mitered design with bottom and top inserted into pre-cut dadoes. It is glued up as one piece, then later ripped in two. Veneers for the marquetry top are cut with a scroll saw, craft knife or similar sharp blade. The design may be traced onto each piece or adjacent pieces of veneer may be laid atop one another and both cut through at once.

The horizontal slot on the front of the box which holds the sliding latch is a saw kerf with a shallower dovetail routed over it. A matching filler rail is glued into this kerf-and-dovetail slot to the left of the latch-hole. To the right, the rail slides in and out, a small notch in its face giving fingernail access. So the grain will match, make this rail using rippings saved from milling the carcass. Cut the saw kerf, then use the dovetail bit to produce the angled profile. A separate keel glued into the saw kerf yields a rail that is the exact male shape to fit the female slot.

To make the hinges, start with four rectangular blocks, each 1" x 1¼" x 3/8" thick. Using a dado blade, mill the slots that create the hinge fingers on a table saw and drill the 1/8"-diameter holes for the hinge pins.

Then round the ends of the fingers by sanding so the hinges will rotate properly. Band saw, carve and sand them to the desired tear-drop shape. Set the hinges in place on the back of the carcass and scribe their outlines. Cut the hinge mortises using a small router and hand chisel.

Note that Upton carefully rounded the rear edges of the top to a level slightly below that of the hinges, giving them a subtly raised effect. Be aware of this while applying the final radius to the box edges with a router with a roundover bit, followed by hand sanding.

ASSEMBLY

The box is glued up with the top and bottom intact. The marquetry on the lid may be applied before or after glue-up. Hinges are completely carved, polished and assembled with small dowels of matching wood to plug the pin-holes, then glued in place on the carcass. The gentle indentations on the sides, which allow fingers to open the lid, are rough-shaped on the 6" x 48" sander by applying the stock directly to the rotating drum, then finished by hand. The dividers are milled, polished and inserted over the velveteen bottom.

MATERIALS: Woodscape, A Marquetry Box

Part	Description	Dimensions	Quantity
A	Front/back	1" x 2⅝" x 12"	2
B	Sides	1" x 2⅝" x 9½"	2
C	Top/bottom	1/4" x 8½" x 11"	2
D	Top veneer	Approx. 8" x 11"	As req'd
E	Latch rail	3/16" x 3/8" x 7"	2
F	Latch rail keel	3/32" x 3/8" x 7"	2
G	Strike dowel	1/4" x 1"	1
H	Hinge stock	3/8" x 1" x 1¼"	4
I	Hinge pin	1/8" x 1"	2
J	Divider	1/8" x 1⅝" x 10½"	2
K	Divider	1/8" x 1⅝" x 7¾"	2

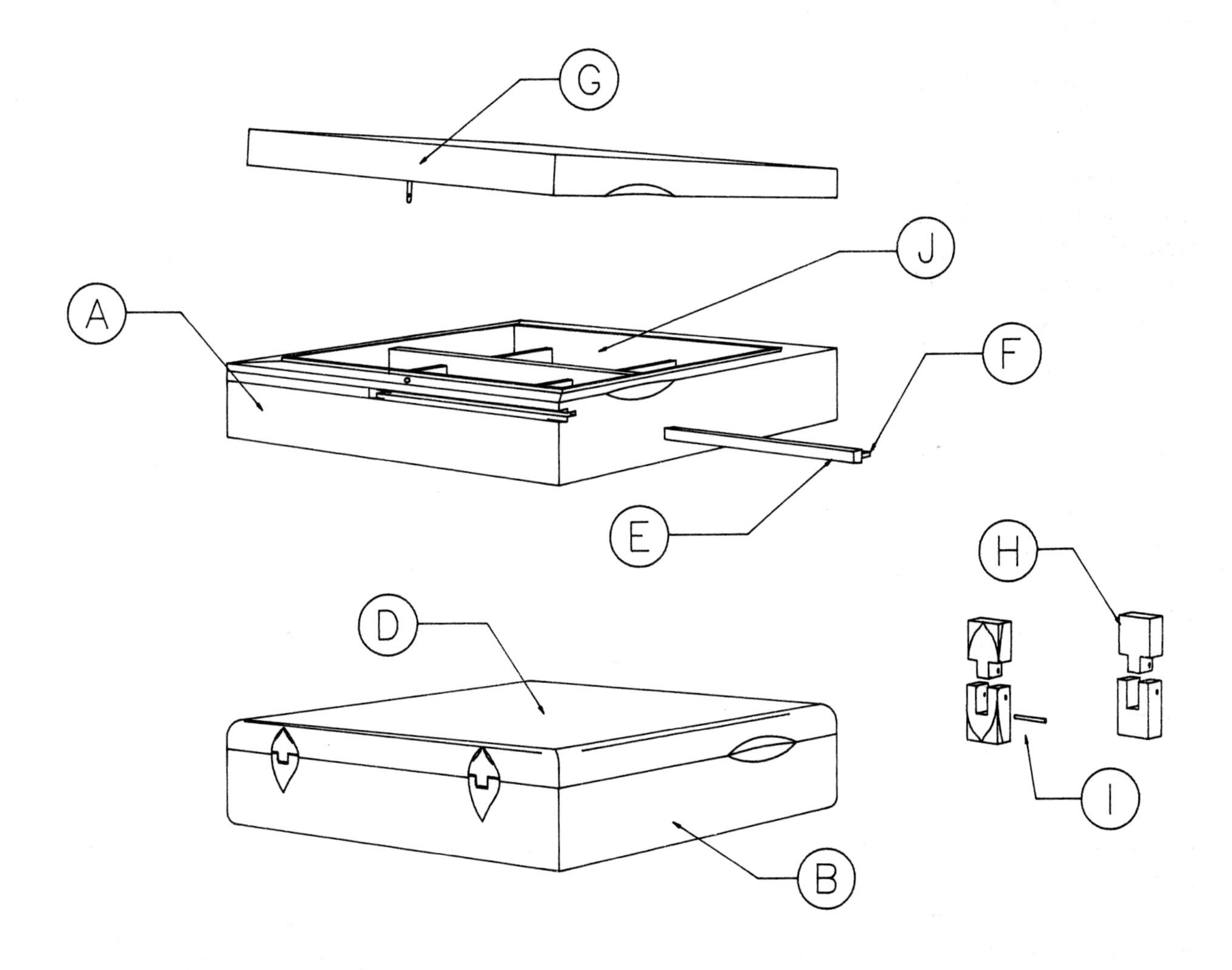

A B C D
E F G H
I J K L
M N O P
Q R S T
U V W X
Y Z

Jacknifed

A Toothpick Box by Jay and Janet O'Rourke

When shaken, these ingenious boxes by Jay and Janet O'Rourke pop out one toothpick at a time. Only three inches long, they simply and thriftily utilize rare and beautiful woods.

WOODS

The O'Rourkes have used figured maple, wenge, cocobolo, tulipwood, purpleheart and satinwood. Like the beautiful hand-crafted jackknives of another day which they resemble, these boxes are perfect showcases for highly-figured, contrasting woods.

MILLING

The two outer sides start as a single block of wood, 1" high and 1/2" thick. Since it is difficult to safely rip pieces as short as 3" on a table saw, use stock about 10" long and mill parts for at least three boxes at a time. Rip the sides 3/32" thick, then crosscut into 3" long matched pairs. The central section of the box, with the hinged arm and the cavity which holds the toothpicks, is fashioned from a 5/16" thick block of contrasting wood. Band sawing this block in the direction of the grain, separate and shape the handle part. Make the fingernail catch in one end of the lower part by drilling at a 45° angle with a 3/16" drill bit. The stock must be firmly clamped to a plate of scrap wood to permit the drill press to make a clean cut. The rectangular cavity is carefully band sawn to prevent breakage of the thin end-grain edges.

Drill holes for the pin hinge in the inside faces of the sides (note that they do not penetrate all the way through) and through the arm. Make a dry assembly of case and innards with the hinge pin in place. Then carefully chisel, shape or sand the parts to achieve proper fit.

ASSEMBLY

Apply a small bead of glue to the inside edges of the central cavity, then assemble with the hinge pin and arm in place. After the glue has dried, shape and polish the completed box on the 6" x 48" sander. Finally, drill a hole at the base of the fingernail catch to allow toothpicks to slide out. The diameter of this hole should be 1/16", or slightly larger than the toothpicks the box will house.

Note: Try whittling home-made toothpicks from leftover scrap.

MATERIALS: Jacknifed, A Toothpick Box

Part	Description	Dimensions	Quantity
A	Side	3/32" x 1" x 3"	2
B	Block for center cavity and handle	5/16" x 1" x 3"	1
C	Hinge pin	3/32" x 7/16"	1
D	Toothpick	1/16" x 2½"	6

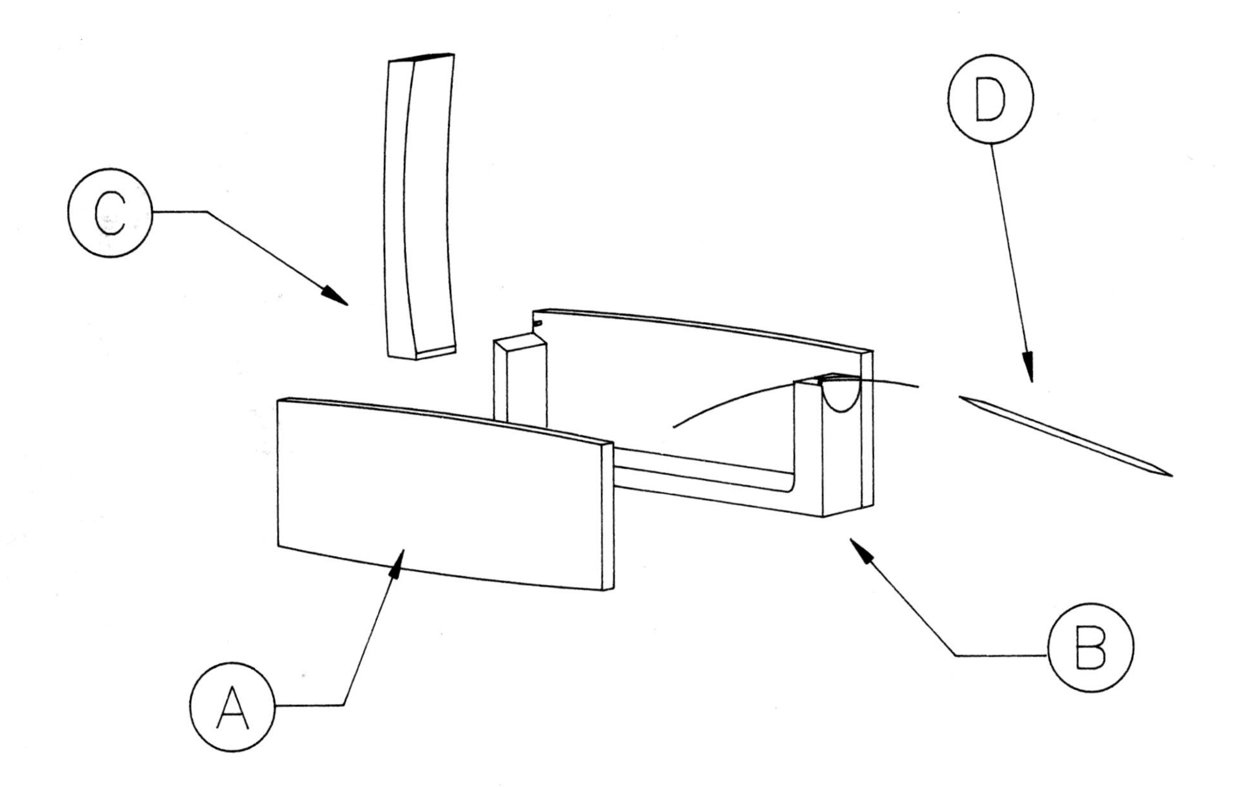

Double Vision

An Inlaid Marquetry Box by Timothy Lydgate

The Hawaiian Islands are home to some of the world's most beautiful woods, and in this group of inlaid boxes Timothy Lydgate has perfected an intricate technique for showcasing them. Conventional marquetry applies a veneer-thin surface design over a solid substrate. The patterns in these boxes, however, are created by laminating solid strips, so the design is visible on both sides.

The following instructions refer to the checkerboard design hinge-top box on the previous page, but the method applies to all the boxes shown.

WOODS

Curly koa, mango, milo, kamani, and ohia are featured, with East Indian rosewood or ebony for accents. Any strong contrasting woods, such as walnut and maple, may also be used. Boxes of this style offer the opportunity to utilize small pieces of highly-figured stock.

MILLING

The top and each of the four sides of this box are fabricated individually, then trimmed to size and mitered for assembly. Each side is made by edge-gluing its five component parts, then flattening on the 6" x 48" sander, trimming to 1¼" width, rabbeting the bottom, and mitering. Slipfeathers are cut in the corners of the box after it is glued up, using a slipfeather jig. Then the bottom and the upper rim edging are added.

To produce the checkerboard portion of the lid, 1/4" x 5/16" x 16" rippings of two contrasting woods (in this design, Indian rosewood and silvery-white sapwood koa) are glued together in black-white-black-white order. The resulting laminate is sanded flat and crosscut into pieces 1/4" wide which are then arranged and re-glued in a checkerboard pattern. Once all parts of the lid have been fabricated in this fashion, they are trimmed and assembled into the final shape. The black and the outer white lid borders are then mitered and applied. Using a quick-set epoxy adhesive also provides an appropriate filler for the tiny gaps present in even the most meticulous work.

ASSEMBLY

The lid is carefully slipfeathered, then sanded to fit the box opening. Because the lid's thinness and multi-laminate makeup tend to minimize climate-caused dimensional changes, an extremely narrow gap — approximately 1/32"— may be left between the lid and the sides.

An invisible pin hinge is used, the pin-holes plugged with small dowels sanded off later. By locating the hinge pin far enough forward, the need for a handle or finger slot is avoided: slight pressure with the thumb on the back edge of the lid opens this box.

MATERIALS: Double Vision, An Inlaid Marquetry Box

Part	Description	Dimensions	Quantity
A	Side laminate part	3/8" x1" x 2¼"	8
	Side laminate part	3/8" x 2¼" x 4½"	4
	Side laminate part	1/4" x 3/8" x 2¼"	8
B	Edge strip for carcass rim	1/8" x 3/8" x 7"	4
C	Bottom	1/8" x 6¼" x 7"	1
D	Carcass slipfeather	1/8" x 1/2" x 1"	16
E	Lid: center medallion	1/4" x 2⅞" x 3½"	1
F	Lid: medallion border	1/16" x 1/4" x 3½"	4
G	Lid: checkerboard strip	1/4" x 5/16" x 16"	4
H	Lid: corner block	1/4" x 1⅛" x 1¼"	8
I	Lid: dark border	1/8" x 1/4" x 6¼"	4
J	Lid: light border	1/16" x 1/4" x 6¼"	4
K	Lid: slipfeather	1/8" x 1¼" x 2¼"	4
L	Hinge pin	1/8" x 3/4"	2
M	Hinge pin plug	1/8" x 3/16"	2
N	Lid support rail	1/8" x 3/16" x 7"	1

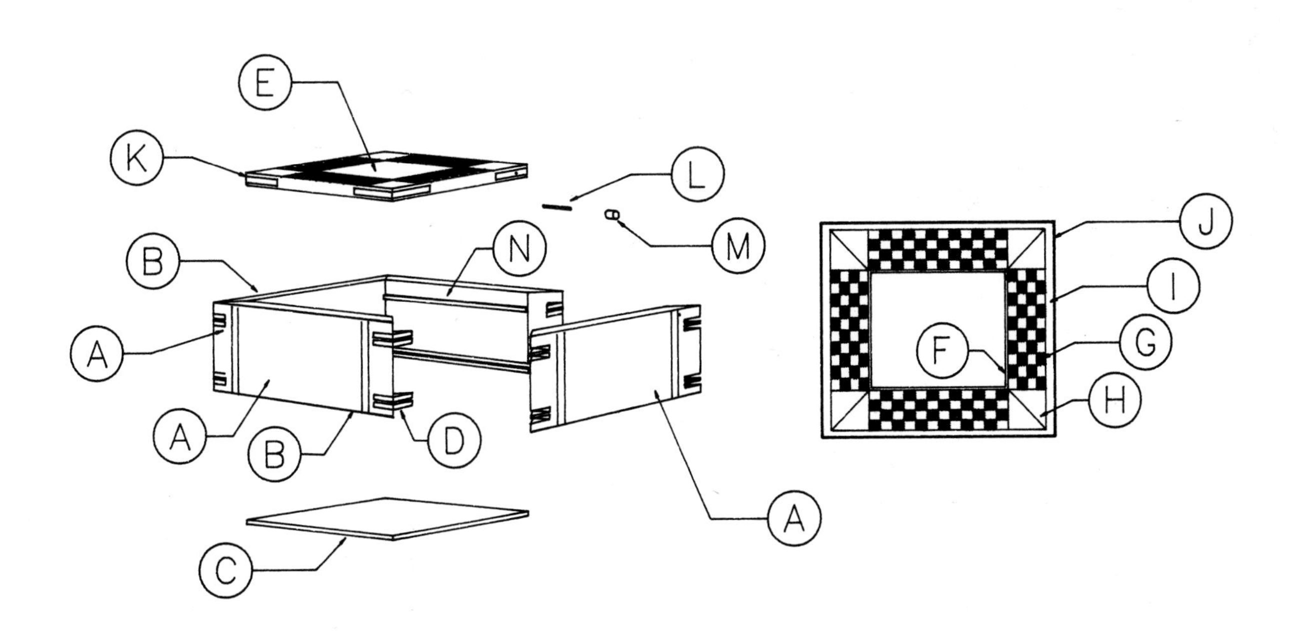

V-Groovy

A Box by Phil and Chris Weber

Phil and Chris Weber's style of box-making is instantly recognizable. Working often in ebony, they have made powerful forms and intriguing intricacy their hallmarks.

WOODS

This design is of ebony and Brazilian rosewood, with brass accents. The dark, grainless surface of ebony and the deliberately simple lines of this design are complementary visual companions. But this box could also be done in a highly-figured wood or in two or three contrasting species.

MILLING

The V-groove that gives the box its name is made with 1/4" square brass tubing, available at hobby shops. First, mill a dado in the two blocks that form the side. Angle it at 45° relative to the vertical plane. This can be done with a V-groove router bit, or by making two cuts at right angles to each other with a table saw blade.

The blade's teeth must be specially ground to produce a flat-bottomed kerf. A 5/16" square piece of ebony or other dark wood the length of the groove is then glued into it and the face of the block is sanded flat. Next, a second, shallower V-groove is cut into the ebony. Glue the brass tubing into that. The unwanted portion of the tubing is sanded off on the 6" x 48" belt sander.

ASSEMBLY

Before assembly, sand and polish all parts. Drill holes for the lid hinge pins, insert them and glue up the box with the lid in place.

MATERIALS: V-Groovy, A Box

Part	Description	Dimensions	Quantity
A	Side	2⅞" x 3½" x 3/4"	2
B	Lid top	1⅝" x 6¾" x 1/4"	1
C	Lid front	7/8" x 6¾" x 1/4"	1
D	Lid front rail	3/8" x 3/8" x 6¾"	1
E	Back	1/4" x 1½" x 6¾"	1
F	Bottom	1/8" x 1⅝" x 6¾"	1
G	Lower front rail	1/2" x 1/4" x 6¾"	1
H	Hinge pin	1/8" x 1/2"	2
I	Brass v-groove	1/4" x 1/4" x 3½"	2
J	Ebony v-groove	5/16" x 5/16" x 3½"	2

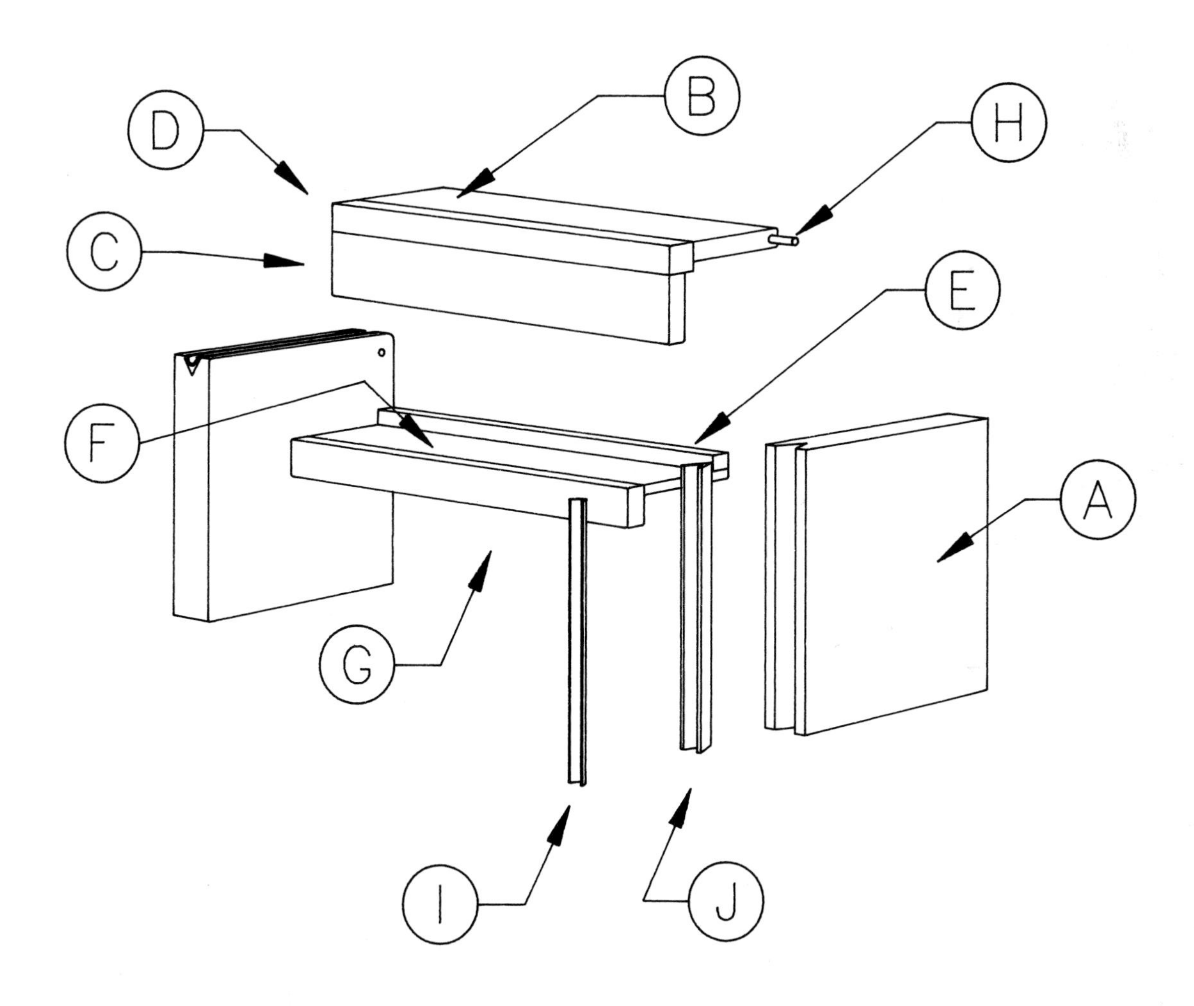

PENTE

Finders Keepers

A Treasure Box by Tony Lydgate

This delightful box recalls the simpler days of childhood: it is exactly the place to store all the treasures collected on the walk home from school.

WOODS

This version is walnut, with the sliding top of maple. An ideal woodworking project for children, this box can also be made in light woods such as oak or pine. Handpainted with love by the youngster who helped create it, the Finders Keepers Box makes a memorable gift.

MILLING

The box is constructed using simple butt joints. The dadoes for the bottom and sliding top are saw kerfs. Rectangular plugs are glued into the tails of the kerfs where they show at the base of the two short sides.

ASSEMBLY

Polish the insides of the parts, then apply glue and clamp with screw-type clamps until dry. The butt joint is one instance where screw clamps are preferable to tape.

MATERIALS: Finders-Keepers, A Treasure Box

Part	Description	Dimensions	Quantity
A	Side	1/2" x 2½" x 9¾"	2
B	Rear end	1/2" x 2½" x 3"	1
C	Front end	1/2" x 2⅛" x 3"	1
D	Bottom	1/8" x 2¾" x 10"	1
E	Sliding lid	1/8" x 2½" x 10¼"	1
F	Saw kerf plug	1/8" x 1/8" x 1/4"	4

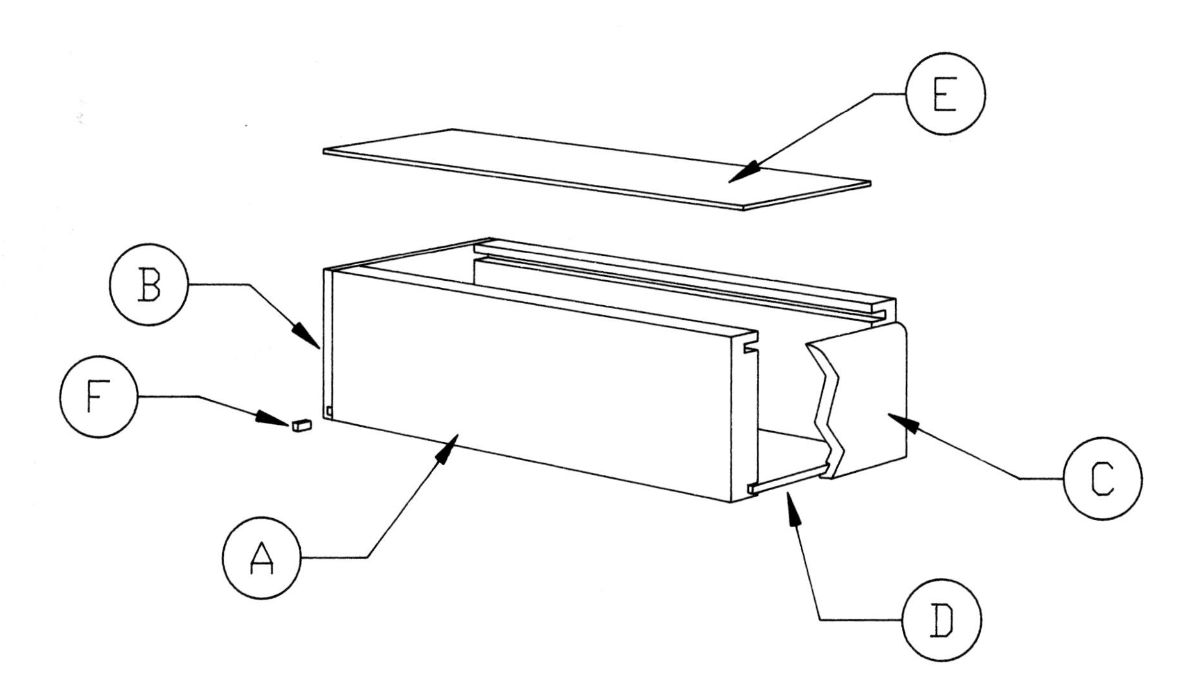

Sailor's Valentine

An Octagonal Box by Tony Lydgate

In the days when ships were powered only by the wind, sailors fashioned gifts for their loved ones from shells gathered on faraway beaches. Today's collectors eagerly seek these "Sailor's Valentines", octagonal boxes with shell designs; even modern interpretations such as this one command high prices.

WOODS

Sailors traditionally used whatever wood was available: oak salvaged from a rotting timber; teak from decking scraps; or anonymous hardwoods harvested at their ships' exotic ports of call. This version is Hawaiian koa.

MILLING

Select stock that will yield eight pieces 5/8" thick, about 4" long and 2⅜" wide. Mill two dadoes, centered vertically on the inside faces, 13/16" and 7/16" wide, then miter the blocks at 22.5°, which is half of a 45° angle. Rabbet both edges for a 1/8" liner of plywood. Make the bookmatched top and bottom of solid wood, from 4⅞" wide stock, 1/8" thick.

ASSEMBLY

First, assemble dry to check the correctness of the angles. For final assembly of the carcass, lay the eight mitered blocks on their faces in a line against a straight edge. Apply to their backs a single piece of 2"-wide tape, about 18" long, then turn the assembly over and put glue in the valleys. Fold this assembly into an octagonal shape and glue in the two 1/8" plywood top and bottom liners.

Then glue on the bookmatched top and bottom. Be sure the grain patterns of the top and bottom are parallel. Use two octagons of 3/4" scrap plywood or particleboard to sandwich the box, and clamp the entire assembly.

After the glue has dried, sand the exterior faces smooth on the 6" x 48" sander. Rip the carcass in two on the table saw. Use the sander to remove the resulting sawmarks in the edges, then cut the hinge mortices using a chisel or the table saw. To ensure that the two halves of the box align properly after they are hinged, screw the hinge onto one half of the box. Apply glue to the underside of the unattached hinge, place the other half of the box in position with the box closed and wait for the glue to dry. Glue does not adhere to brass very well but, with care, the glued hinge will stay in position long enough to mark the location of its screw holes.

There are as many possible patterns for the seashell design as there are varieties of seashells in the ocean. One way to approach the challenge is to research 18th and 19th Century seafarers' creations at the library. Historical models range from simple "To My Sweetheart" patterns to dazzling intricacies of shape, color and surface texture.

Rigorous symmetry distinguishes the traditional designs. Each half of the box is internally symmetrical and the two halves are mirror images. Small shells are used for the background. Larger and more brightly-colored ones are postioned on the four compass points.

Before glue seals the commitment , try out various designs on paper templates the same size as the finished octagon.

Mill the two Plexiglas covers and the sixteen trim strips. After the box has been oiled and waxed, glue in the shell pattern. Finally, insert the Plexiglas and glue on the trim strips.

MATERIALS: Sailor's Valentine, An Octagonal Box

Part	Description	Dimensions	Quantity
A	Side	5/8" x 2⅜" x 3⅞"	8
B	Top/bottom liner	1/8" x 8⅝" x 8⅝"	2
C	Top/bottom	1/8" x 9½" x 9½"	2
D	Trim strip	1/8" x 5/16" x 3⅝"	16
E	Plexiglas cover	1/8" x 8⅝" x 8⅝"	2
F	Brass hinge	1½" x 5/8"	1
G	Brass shutter hook	—	1

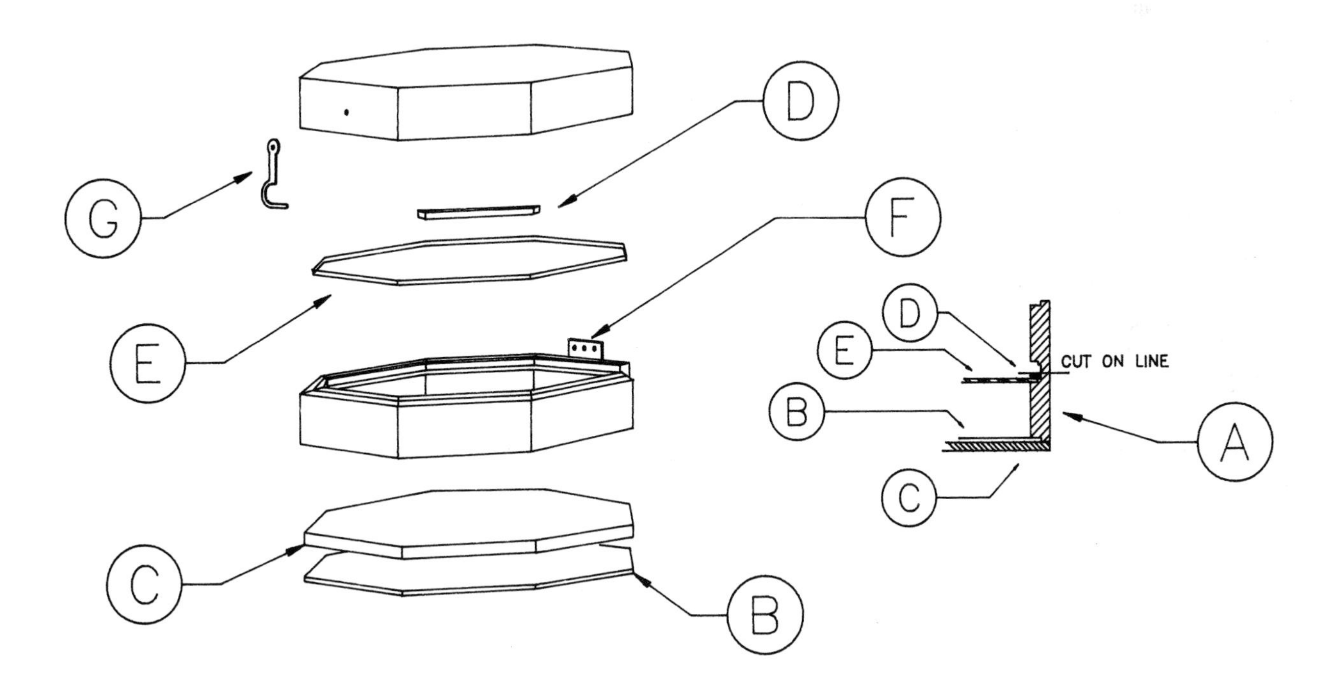

19th Century

A Tambour Box by Richard Rinehart

South Dakota woodworker Richard Rinehart's intimately scaled box conceals its secrets with slats of wood attached to a flexible canvas backing known as a tambour. This plain but graceful style of closure was widely used in turn-of-the-century furniture, particularly for covering desktops, thus its more familiar name of "roll-top".

WOODS

Rinehart has selected birdseye maple, with a drawer front, handle and side detailing of sateen.

MILLING

The two sides are band sawed to outline form from 1/2" stock. The 1/8" tambour track, the dadoes for the shelf and drawer rails and the rabbet for the bottom are then milled using a router.

Rinehart's tambour bears the mark of a master craftsman: a grain pattern continuous across the slats. This was accomplished by ripping a board into strips 3/8" wide, then slicing the strips to 3/16" thickness to yield the slats.

ASSEMBLY

All the carcass parts, including the tambour slats, are sanded and polished. The tambour is assembled by gently but firmly holding the slats, upside down and in final shape and order, flat on the work table in a clamping jig. Apply a thin bead of glue along the midline of each slat in the direction of the grain, then lay on medium weight 100% cotton canvas. Spread out the glue with gentle rubbing. Leave approximately a 1/2" margin between the edge of the canvas and the sides of the box to prevent interference with the operation of the tambour.

After the tambour has dried, make a dry assembly of the box without glue. Correct the edges of the tambour by sanding or scraping until it runs smoothly on its track. The entire carcass, tambour in place, is then glued up. Attach the turned handle to the first slat, then fabricate and install the drawer. When oiling, avoid getting oil on the tambour canvas, as this may weaken it over time.

MATERIALS: 19th Century, A Tambour Box

Part	Description	Dimensions	Quantity
A	Side	1/2" x 6¾" x 9½"	2
B	Bottom	3/8" x 3⅜" x 11¾"	1
C	Shelf	1/4" x 7¾" x 11½"	1
D	Tambour slat	3/16" x 3/8" x 11¼"	23
E	Tambour handle slat	3/16" x 3/4" x 11¼"	1
F	Handle	3/4" x 3/4" x 1"	1
G	Drawer side	1/4" x 2" x 6 13/16"	2
H	Drawer back	1/4" x 2" x 10½"	1
I	Drawer front liner	1/4" x 2" x 10⅞"	1
J	Drawer front	1/4" x 2½" x 11⅛"	1
K	Drawer side trim	1/8" x 2" x 2½"	2
L	Drawer bottom	1/8" x 6¾" x 10⅝"	1
M	Drawer rail	1/4" x 1/2" x 5"	2
N	Tambour canvas	10" x 10¼"	1

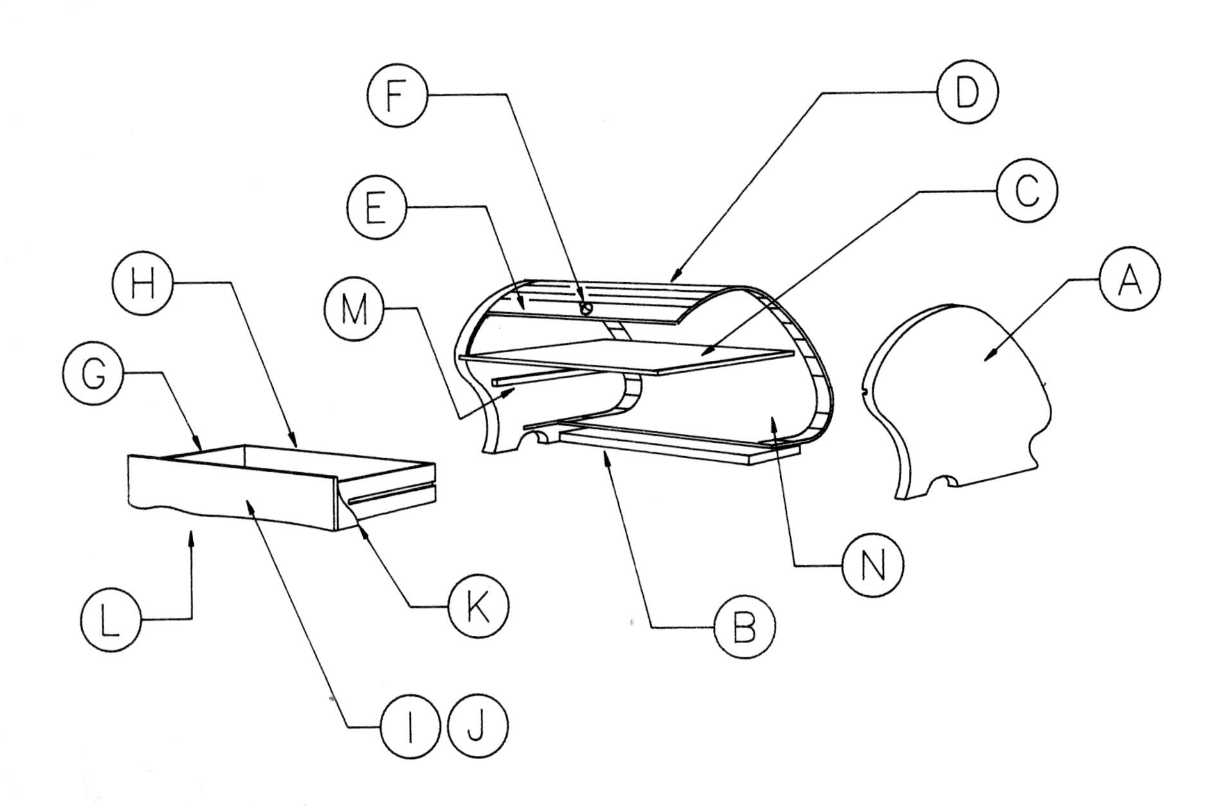

Contemplation

A Zen Sandbox by Tony Lydgate

The art of contemplation plays an important role in the philosophy of many cultures. From ancient times to the present, Zen masters have raked organic patterns in gardens of sand and stone. These patterns are an aid to meditation on matters ranging from universal harmony to the insignificance of human volition.

WOODS

This box is created from birdseye maple, with Indian rosewood feet and a cocobolo rake. A true existentialist recognizes that no wood is superior to any other, so any combination will do.

MILLING

The four sides are mitered, and a slot is milled for the bottom. The eight pieces that will form the feet are mitered on one end. After the carcass is glued up, including the feet, its sides are ripped on the table saw at an angle of 12°, then polished on the sander. The rake is made by slotting a 5/16" thick piece of hardwood with the table saw blade at 1/16" spacing, then crosscutting at a 16° angle.

MATERIALS: Contemplation, A Zen Sandbox

Part	Description	Dimensions	Quantity
A	Side	7/8" x 1½" x 14"	2
B	End	7/8" x 1½" x 8"	2
C	Side foot	3/16" x 1¼" x 2¼"	4
D	End foot	3/16" x 1¼" x 1¼"	4
E	Bottom	1/8" x 7½" x 13½"	1
F	Rake	5/16" x 2" x 3"	1

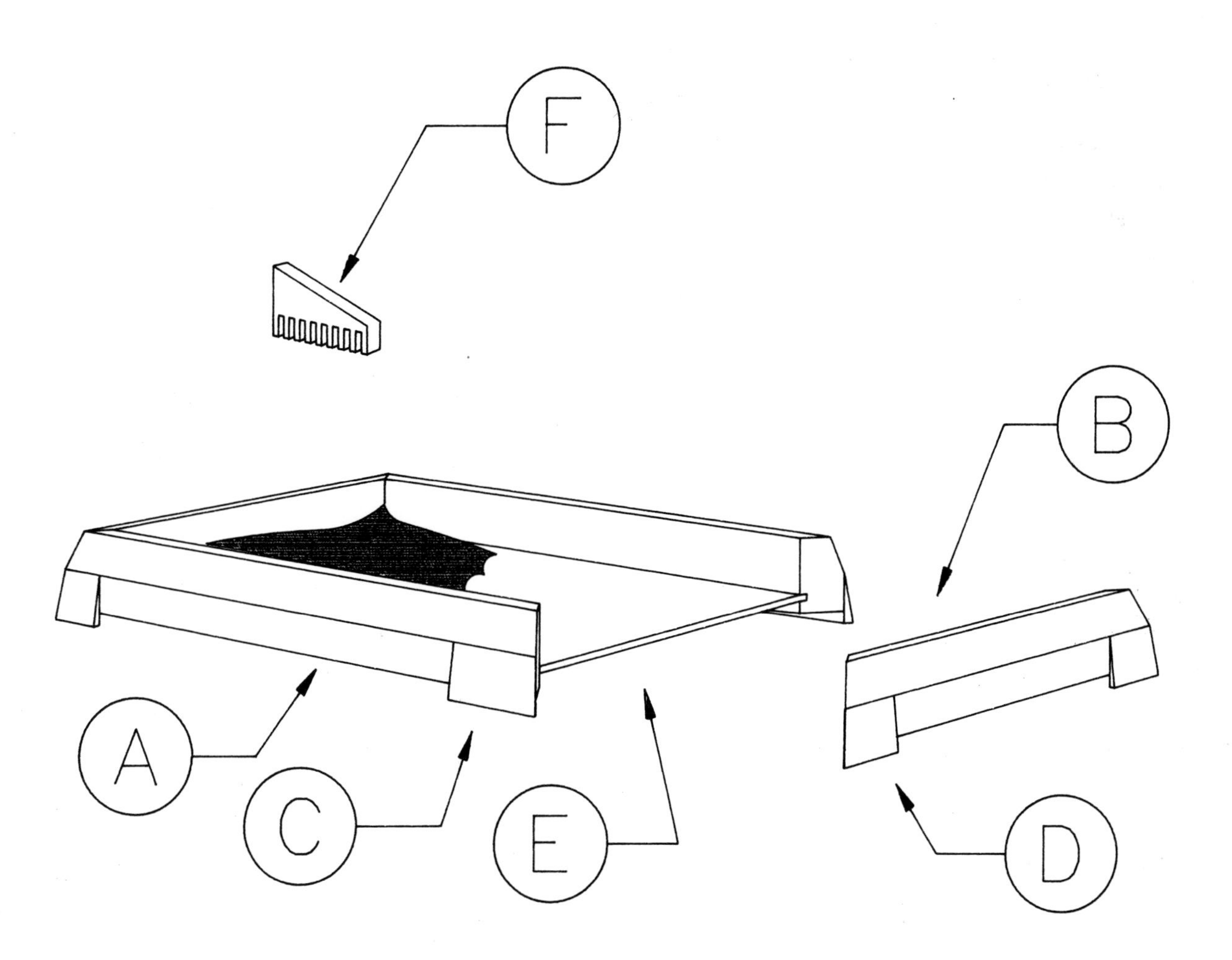

Garden Grace

A Planter by Tony Lydgate

Beautiful woods are seldom used in conjunction with fresh flowers or plants because the water needs of the latter present a risk to glue joints and fine finishes. This planter design eliminates the risk by using waterproof glue, exterior varnish and metal pans. Now superb woods and their natural botanical cousins can once again complement each other.

WOODS

The example shown is cherry. Other light woods such as maple, pine, fir, birch and alder, or dark woods such as walnut and mahogany, can also harmonize with the type of plant or flower to be displayed.

MILLING

The dimensions are based on 8" square metal baking pans, 2" deep. These are available in any hardware store or supermarket. Since pan size determines planter size, obtain the pans first and modify the project's dimensions to accommodate their size and shape. Use the drill press to punch five 1/4" diameter holes in the bottom of the upper pan, which holds the plants.

After the parts for the upper and lower boxes are blanked out, mill 3/8" dadoes 1/8" deep on each inside face. Polish-sand the insides and give the upper edges an eased radius. Glue in the rails that will support the pans, then mill the miters on the table saw.

ASSEMBLY

Glue up the lower box with the feet, using waterproof glue. The upper box must be glued with the lower pan in place. Do not glue the two boxes to each other. This simplifies emptying the lower pan, which catches water draining from the upper one. Before adding soil and plants, cover the bottom of the upper pan with a layer of small rocks or gravel to prevent soil from washing through the drainage holes.

Finish Note: To protect against moisture, apply three coats of exterior grade waterproof polyurethane or comparable varnish to all surfaces of the planter.

MATERIALS: Garden Grace, A Planter

Part	Description	Dimensions	Quantity
A	Lower box side	3/4" x 1½" x 10¾"	4
B	Upper box side	3/4" x 3½" x 10"	4
C	Leg	3/4" x 1" x 1¾"	4
D	Pan rail	3/8" x 3/8" x 8½"	8
E	Metal pan	2" x 8¼" x 8¼"	2

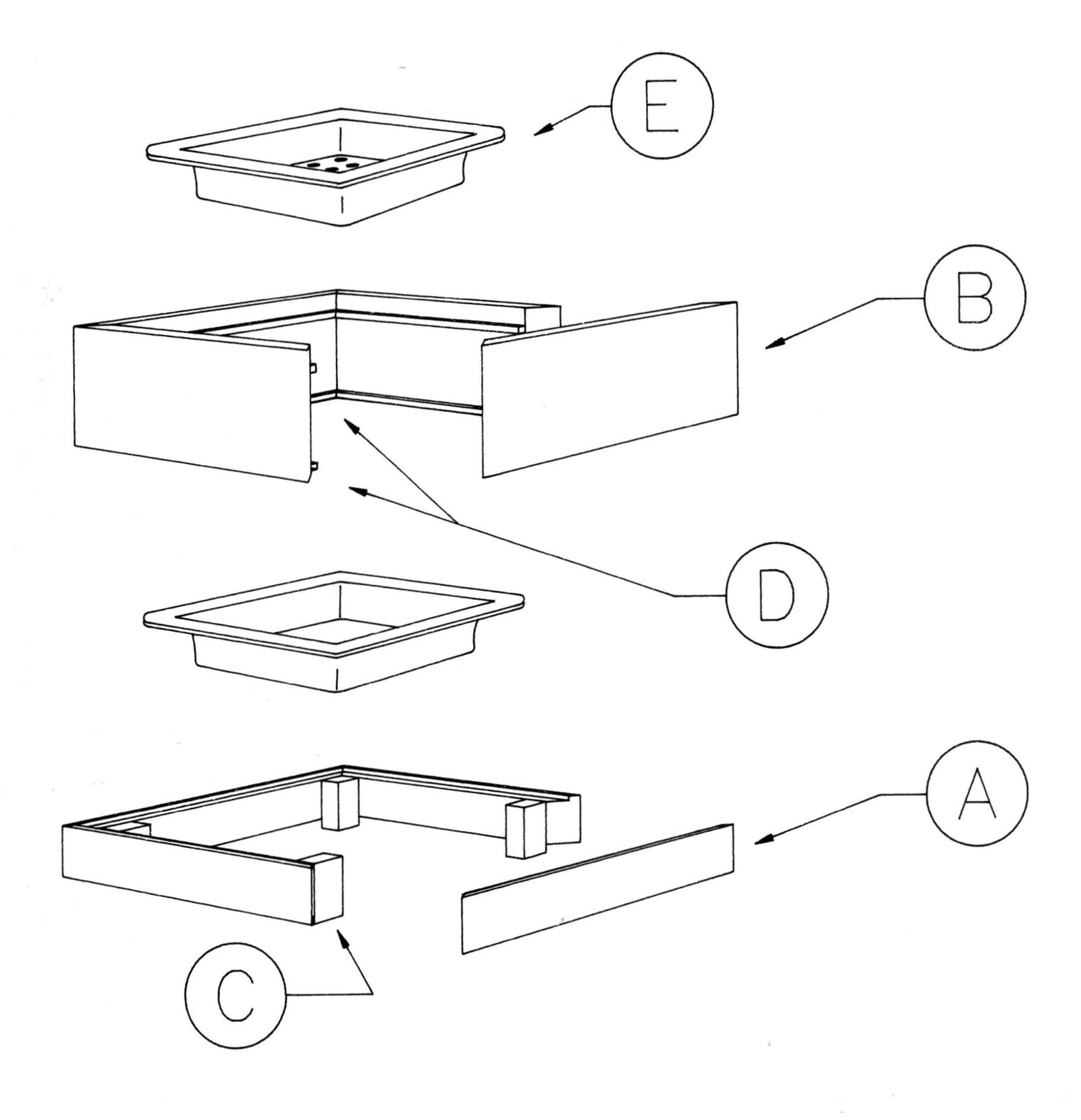

Dandy Candy

A Candy Dispenser by Kevin Lasher

Everyone remembers that not so very long ago a nickel would buy a handful of delights from the candy machine with the crank. Kevin Lasher revives this familiar contraption as a dramatic A-frame. The candies tumble noisily down through a field of dowels into the cups below, adding to the fun of this design.

WOODS

The candy dispenser is of mahogany and tiger maple, one of the many combinations, including purpleheart and satinwood, that Lasher uses. The bright candy colors invite experimentation with brightly colored woods.

MILLING

The 15° cuts at the peak and 75° cuts at the base of the A-frame sides are made by using the miter fence on the table saw. The 16° bevel cuts on the base and cup block, in contrast, are done by angling the saw blade. The pattern for the field of 1/8" dowels through which the candies tumble is drawn on the back stock, then drilled on the drill press.

With the stock placed at an angle, use a Forstner bit or hole saw to make openings in the A-frame sides for the turning handle. The sides are rabbeted for the back. The Plexiglas front fits into a saw kerf dado.

The turning mechanism releasing the candies is a 1½"-diameter dowel, with triangular handles attatched to each end. A drill press makes the oval depression where each candy is captured. Make the cup block into which the candies fall by routing oval cuts entirely through the block. If the inside edges are too rough, clean them up with a small sanding sleeve on the drill press.

The rear underside of the block is then band sawed at an angle and sanded flat. A wedge-shaped block is glued on to produce the sloping floor.

ASSEMBLY

Polish and glue up the A-frame, as well as the back and the vertical piece that goes between the two sides at the apex. Then use a band saw to slice off the top of the triangle. Smooth both edges of the cut with a sanding block. Glue on facing strips that together equal the thickness of the saw cut. Drill holes for and insert the two 1/4" dowels that secure the top. After final sanding and finish, glue in the tumble dowels (see photo) and insert the Plexiglas front.

The cup block and A-frame assembly are attached to the base from underneath with countersunk screws. Finally, insert the turning dowel and glue on its triangular handles.

MATERIALS: Dandy Candy, A Candy Dispenser

Part	Description	Dimensions	Quantity
A	Side	7/8" x 3" x 18"	2
B	Apex block	3/8" x 3" x 4"	1
C	Back	3/4" x 7½" x 14"	1
D	Front	1/8" x 7½" x 14"	1
E	Cup block	1" x 4" x 8"	1
F	Base	7/8" x 6" x 10½"	1
G	Turning dowel	1½" x 9½"	1
H	Turning dowel handle	3/8" x 3¼"	2
I	Top dowel	1/4" x 1½"	2
J	Tumble stick	1/8" x 1½"	40
K	Top cut liner strip	1/16" x 1" x 3"	4

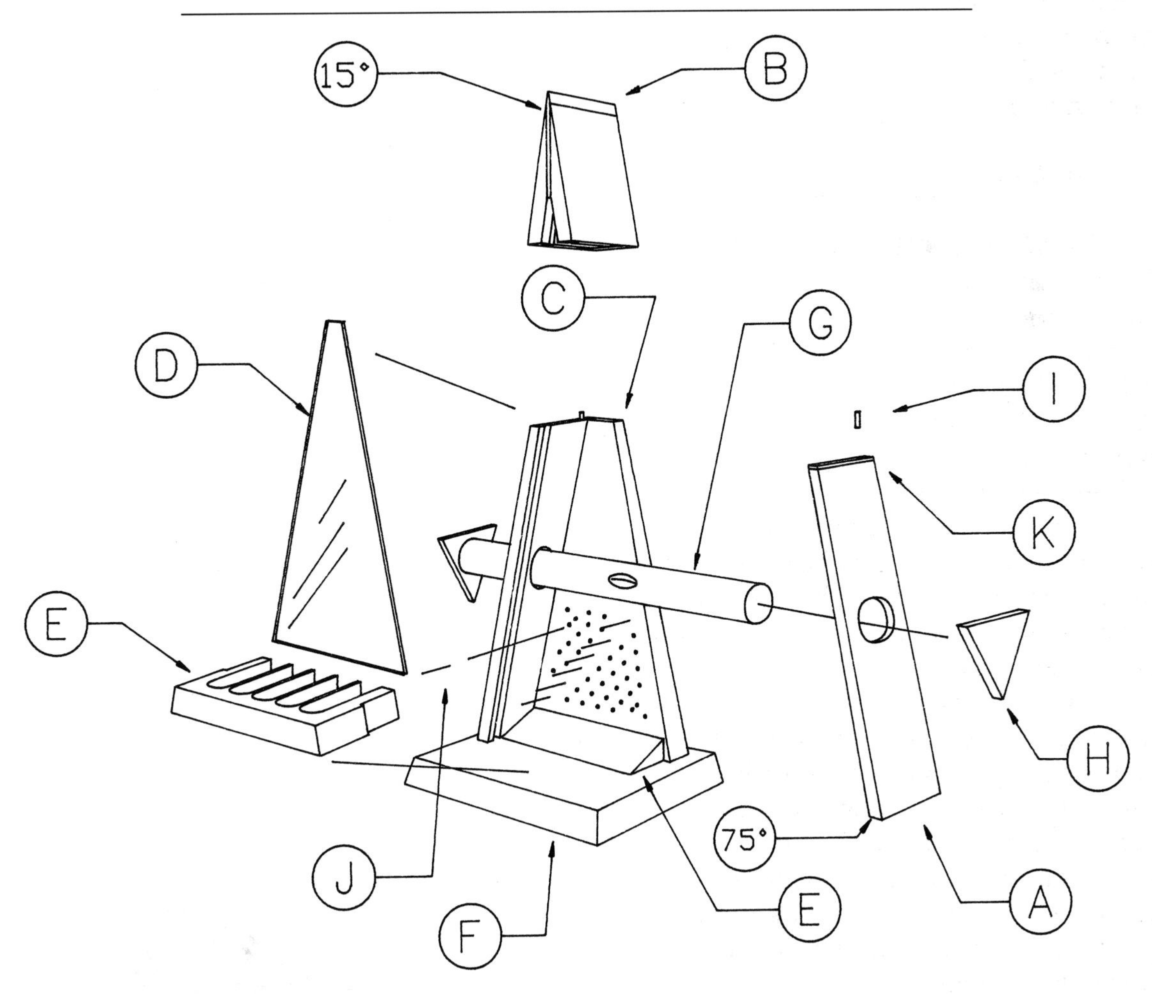

Subtle Spheres

Lathe-turned Vessels by Michael Mode

The elegance and delicacy of these vessels by Michael Mode mark them as the work of a master woodturner.

WOODS

Created from maple burl, the vessels have rosewood collars.

MILLING

Mode turns the forms "green"; the rough shapes are machined on the lathe while the wood is nearly as moist as when the tree was harvested. After this initial shaping, Mode allows the pieces to air dry for six to eight weeks. This drying reduces the moisture content enough to prevent further warping or distortion as the wood dries and settles. The pieces are then returned to the lathe for final shaping and polishing.

The collars are turned from blocks of rosewood glued to scrap wood. Their lower edges are slightly bevelled, as are the inner edges of the vessels. The result is virtually seamless attachment.

A more elaborate version of Mode's lidded vessels appears in the Gallery section, page 123.

MATERIALS: Subtle Spheres, Lathe-turned Vessels

Part	Description	Dimensions	Quantity
A	Body	4" x 4" x 4"	1
B	Collar	1" x 3½" x 3½"	1
C	Lid	1" x 3" x 3"	1

Gallery
Masterpieces In Wood

PREFACE

A true marriage of material with form and function yields an object that rises far above mere utility. The thirteen pieces in this Gallery are all boxes, yet more than boxes.

Their evocative and intriguing forms and surfaces invite one to touch. Their massive sculptural qualities belie their scale, for none are enormous.

The master box-makers represented in this Gallery of masterpieces are among the finest in the United States today. They probe the endless complexities of deceptively simple boxes, opening new design paths with each piece.

Perhaps their boldness will inspire the reader, leading to masterpieces of the future.

Mesa Arizona

Tony Lydgate

Tony Lydgate

Tony Lydgate traces his love of wood to the rocky coast of his native New England where, as a young beachcomber, he would bring home lumber washed ashore from the decks of passing ships.

The boy scraped off the sand, salt and weathered exterior, usually to discover spruce or oak. From time to time, especially in winter, he would find prized boards of mahogany or rosewood. The natural beauty of the wood pleased him and the first use he made of it was to teach himself to carve. Captivated by curves and serifs, he spent hours incising words into the planks.

The young craftsman did not know of specially designed carvers' gouges. Instead, he painstakingly cut into dense hardwoods using the only tool he possessed, a straight-blade half-inch chisel.

Lydgate's early fascination with wood was a precursor to his becoming the master craftsman he is today. His inventive craft and furniture designs have earned him a national reputation.

Since 1978, he has been a regular exhibitor at the American Craft Council's annual shows, where he has twice served as an elected juror. His jewelry boxes, functional crafts, sculptural containers and furniture are exhibited at fine galleries throughout the United States.

As a crafts advocate and educator, Lydgate extols the importance of the hand-made. He is particularly concerned with helping creative people develop their work "by establishing a sound business basis to support it." His articles, letters and commentary on crafts and crafts marketing have appeared in *The Crafts Report, American Craft Magazine, The Woodworker's Journal* and *Fine Woodworking*. He was elected to a three-year term as a Director of the American Craft Association in 1992.

Lydgate says his first experience with box-making came with two projects built while he was in college: a harpsichord and an intricately veneered backgammon set.

"Their insides were completely different," he says. "One contained musical strings, the other had dice and a veneered playing surface, but both hid their secrets from you when they were closed. This secrecy, this hiding, was what got me interested in boxes."

Some of the boxes Lydgate designed to explore this interest are quite simple and intended to hold common household objects like playing cards, pens and pencils or jewelry. Others test the strength and versatility of wood, their compelling shapes leaving the question of function to the collector.

In addition to several of his own pieces, *The Art of Making Elegant Wood Boxes* features Lydgate's personal selection of the best designs from some of the most prominent professional box-makers in the country today.

Lydgate's showcased Gallery piece, "Mesa Arizona", exemplifies his recognizable touch, with emphasis on clean lines and the use of spectacular natural woods. Both functional and visually appealing, the box offers a fresh treatment of the Southwestern artistic tradition.

His "Koa Treasury", shown on the following pages, is a stately interpretation of Oriental architecture. At once delicate and powerful, the piece demonstrates the drama inherent in contrasting woods.

Koa Treasury

Tony Lydgate

City in a Dream
Po Shun Leong

Po Shun Leong

Po Shun Leong creates drama and surprise by carving woods into opulent objects. His miniature cabinets are an invitation to the fingers and a feast for the eyes. Recently he began a sculptural series exploring forms which move and fold into themselves.

Leong taught himself the ways of woodworking. The results are architecturally inspired cabinets, jewelry chests, furniture and sculptures which have been internationally exhibited.

Each piece combines Mexican, classical Greek, Roman and Gothic design and what Leong terms "Oriental complexity". Born in London, Leong traveled to Mexico and lived there for 15 years, designing buildings and absorbing the indigenous culture.

Becoming interested in sculpture, Leong decided to move to the United States. He made a natural transition to cabinets when he moved to Southern California in 1981. "I do plans as if they were buildings with floors and a roof," he says.

Drawing on architectural traditions from Europe, ancient Greece and Rome, the Americas and China, he employs a variety of architectural elements — miniature columns, stairways, arches and bridges. Some pieces have built-in lights, reflecting Leong's work as a stage designer.

Leong often uses exotic woods such as mahogany, koa and rosewood, but favors domestic woods including cherry burl, walnut and olive obtained from a local tree trimmer. Closed, his cabinets present a solid structural facade. A closer inspection reveals the secret pivoting compartments. His signed, dated pieces range in height from six inches to six feet.

Numerous publications have featured articles about Leong's work, including the *New York Times; L.A. Times, Chicago Tribune, China Daily News, American Craft Magazine, Fine Woodworking, Metropolitan Home, Interiors* and *Art Today.*

He has exhibited his pieces at the Museum of Modern Art, Mexico City; Royal Drawing Society, London; American Craft Museum, New York; Atlanta International Museum of Art & Design; Mint Museum, North Carolina; Huntsville Museum of Art, Alabama; and the Smithsonian, Washington, D.C.

"Wood is very forgiving," says Leong. "If I make a mistake, I can turn it into a success."

Leong's successes result in complex boxes revealing evocative and mysterious inner scenes. This signature touch is most eloquently displayed in the artist's Gallery piece. Intended to interact with the observer, "City in a Dream" changes as its parts are moved.

Shoji
John Reed Fox

John Reed Fox

In this age of mass production, the process of crafting one-of-a-kind objects has become a ceremony of renewal and connection for both the maker and the purchaser. A love for this ceremony draws John Reed Fox to woodworking. In harmony with the nature of the art, he prefers traditional Japanese hand tools, including saws and planes manufactured in Japan.

"For me," John says, "the relationship between craftsperson, materials, tools and method is the most essential element in my work."

John has been designing and building unique furniture since 1979. Now living and working in Massachusetts, he is a native of White Plains, New York. Though he briefly attended the University of Chicago, John is a self-taught woodworker.

He names Japanese housewares and architecture as major influences. Their graceful merging of the functional with the decorative is reflected in John's pieces, which are clean and elegant. Like the traditional Japanese craftsman, he treats joinery as both a structural and a decorative element, making even the smallest details pleasing to the eye.

John's work has been published in *The New York Times*, *American Craft Magazine* and *Woodwork Magazine*. His pieces have appeared in such shows as "Orientalism" at the Franklin Parrash Gallery, Washington, D.C.; the Philadelphia Craft Show and the A.C.C. Craft Fair at West Springfield in Massachusetts.

In the spirit of the Japanese artists he admires, John either oils his pieces or leaves them unfinished. The natural beauty of the surfaces offers a satisfying visual and a tactile experience. John prefers domestic woods such as cherry and walnut, "for their subtlety", a characteristic quality of Japanese art as well.

"Shoji", the box shown in the Gallery, is contemporary, yet serenely timeless in its use of translucent shoji screens. Large versions of these paper screens have been essential to privacy in Japanese homes for hundreds of years. Their lightness provides an elegant backdrop for the intricate design of the doors and drawer pulls.

GOTHAM

Of Colors

Pamela Morin

Pamela Morin

Dana Kellog

In Pamela Morin's world, lizards who wear high heels may have clocks in their middles, and cabinets may have faces. The colors are hot and intense. "I like to transform traditional pieces, such as boxes, through the use of whimsical, bold surface decoration," says Pamela.

The New York artist's background is in graphic, jewelry and furniture design. The years of jewelry design are reflected in her use of metal rings, hoops and dots. She combines them with plywood cut-outs, creating multi-layered appliques on furniture, boxes and other objects.

Pamela's major inspiration is folk art, with its melding of form and function. She owns a vast collection of it, including quilts, masks and Latin American and Far Eastern shrine figures. Objects one lives with should be "fun, full of color and life, and make us smile, if not laugh."

Because her boxes are painted, Pamela prefers smooth woods with no grain, such as poplar or maple. She says boxes contain a delightful element of surprise because there are insides to them as well as outsides.

Pamela paints her pieces with bright acrylics and adds hoops, rings and metal dots: contemporary meets primitive. This meeting inspired the name of her studio, "Contemporary Primitives".

Pamela's work has been featured in publications such as *House Beautiful*, *New York Magazine*, *Home Magazine* and *American Home*. She has also exhibited at numerous galleries and museums, including the Whitney Museum, New York; the St. Louis Museum of Art, St. Louis, Missouri; the Museum of Contemporary Arts, Los Angeles, California, and the High Museum, Atlanta, Georgia.

Her Gallery pieces, grouped under the title "Of Colors", exemplify the graphic boldness, imagination and whimsy of Pamela's work. Like the folk art she admires, they intrigue, charm, and bring a smile.

Orb with Amethyst

Michael Mode

Michael Mode

Michael Mode's first experience using a wood lathe involved creating small wooden jars with lids. The emphasis should be on lids, he says. Turned and lidded wooden vessels have became "almost an obsession" for the Vermont woodworker.

Extracting a globular form from a block of wood means cutting away the entire center portion and wasting much beautiful material, especially in highly-figured woods. Mode began putting lids on his bowls not only to save what would normally be tossed aside but also for an even more compelling reason.

"Maybe the lids appealed to me by suggesting something hidden, something interior, and indeed, most people when they first see a lidded vessel immediately remove lid and look inside," he says. "Whatever the reason, I'm still making lids 17 years later."

Lidded vessels demand more technical expertise than simple bowls: slight warpage will cause the lid to stick, so Mode turns his pieces green, air-dries and kiln-dries them, then turns them a second time to reach the final form. Finishing insides just as carefully as outsides has always mattered to him.

Lately Mode has begun adding natural crystals such as quartz, amethyst and citrine to the tops of the turned wood vessels. "For me, they go together and the combination may actually lead me away from lidded forms into purely sculptural shapes," he says. "Whatever I create, I do it because I imagine an object I've never seen and I want strongly to bring it into existence."

Rose McNulty

His Gallery piece, "Orb with Amethyst", is a rich interplay of rounded forms. Topped with a glimmering jewel, the vessel indeed suggests something hidden — perhaps a royal relic or the clue to some great mystery.

BY THE SESSIONS CLOCK CO.. FORESTVILLE. CONN.

Baby Grand

Phil Weber

Ariel

Phil Weber

Phil Weber

The average New York City native might not consider horseshoeing as a career, but Phil Weber is anything but average. After a few years of college in his home state, he entered farrier school. "I knew nothing about horses and soon figured out I was on the wrong end of them as a horseshoer," says Phil.

That experience did teach him that he liked working with his hands, so he decided to investigate another craft — this time, woodworking, with an emphasis on boxes. Other than one or two basic courses taken since he began woodworking in 1976, Phil is essentially a self-taught box-maker.

By 1982, he and his wife were in North Carolina, where Phil formally opened his woodworking shop. A 1986 move to Maine, where he felt much more at home, was a boost to his creativity. He still lives and works there.

He has been exhibiting his work since 1984 in American Craft Enterprise shows at West Springfield, Massachusetts, and Baltimore, Maryland. The prestigious Philadelphia Craft Show has accepted Phil's pieces three times, awarding him first prize in 1991.

He also sells his finely-crafted boxes at galleries in more than twelve states, including New York, Illinois and California.

Though he enjoys working with spalted maple, satinwood and Bolivian rosewood, Phil's favorite is ebony. In addition to this wood's excellent quality, its black color, while dramatic, does not overwhelm the design and complements other woods and metals used with it.

Bob Barrett

Though Phil names architectural styles, Oriental art and Art Deco as influences, he states his artistic goals very simply: "I want to create something people will find beautiful to look at and touch. Something for someone to hand down to the next generation. Pretty complicated, isn't it?"

Yet, box-making is a complicated art, in which Phil excels. His first Gallery piece, "Baby Grand", is an intricate interplay of angles and levels of contrasting woods. The second Gallery design shown here, "Ariel", is classically elegant, even in its simplicity. Both should fulfill the box-maker's desire to create a treasured heirloom that is also beautiful.

Monument

Michael Elkan

Michael Elkan

Michael Elkan respects the twists and turns in a tree and utilizes that character to create rough-hewn yet elegant works of art. A wood's unique characteristics and grain patterns suggest to the artist what that piece will become.

"I may look at a slice off the tree for years before the furniture within reveals itself to me," says Elkan, whose studio and home are

in Oregon.

Elkan had a few woodworking skills when he began experimenting with making furniture 13 years ago in his garage. He found he had an appreciation for the design within the wood itself. Discovering opportunity in knotted burls, he sought to preserve the wood's natural beauty. Among his favorites are native woods such as maple burl, walnut, horse chestnut, alder burl, redwood, white oak burl and myrtle wood.

To make a piece, Elkan begins with a single slab or hunk of wood, which has been slowly air-dried and finished off in a kiln. "Wood doesn't force easily; it won't bend into something that it doesn't want to be," he says. For instance, the rockers on one of Elkan's signature rocking chairs are cut from the tree's natural bulges.

The Michael Elkan Studio's decorative burl boxes and furniture, some pieces retaining natural rough bark edges, are sold in galleries in New York, London, Austria, Australia, Japan and Bermuda. Elkan is well known to collectors and craftsmen on the East Coast as a premier designer of handcrafted furniture.

The road to Elkan's woodworking design career spans the United States from coast to coast. He began work in the family's clothing store at age 10. By 18, he was a salesman for children's clothing. He moved on to join a New York sweater manufacturer and, by age 25, was designing knitwear. But at age 30, Elkan left the high-pressure environment, drove north through Canada, then finally settled in Oregon.

Surrounded by wild loveliness at the foothills of the Cascades, Elkan began coaxing their hidden designs from burls and other wood. His work proved popular at the Oregon State Fair in 1979, so he became serious about woodworking. He crafted rocking chairs, then dining chairs and cabinets.

"Each piece is made to be the only one of its kind, to have the harmony of still living, almost growing form," Elkan says of his work.

The mastery evident in all of his boxes, cabinets and larger pieces of furniture is not due solely to expert mechanics or unique joinery. It emerges from a desire for expression and a sensitivity to what the wood wishes to become. "I think that is what makes each piece a blend of man and nature, which is sometimes magical," Elkan says.

"Magical" aptly describes Elkan's Gallery piece, "Monument". Like a slab hewn from a mountain of hieroglyphics, the wood box reminds one of solid, weathered stone. But closer inspection reveals shrouded doors and caverns of unexpected shape.

Sand Whispers
Charles Cobb

Charles Cobb

Charles Cobb produces highly-crafted, functional sculpture from his California studio. For the last few years, he has concentrated on building uncommon containers in addition to tables, desks, handrails and mantles.

A self-taught woodworker since 1975, Cobb also holds a Bachelor of Fine Arts degree from the Art Center College of Design at Pasadena, California. He has juried more than 30 shows and fairs since 1969 and his work has been seen in publications such as *Northern California Home and Garden, Woodwork, Peninsula Magazine, Furniture Today* and *Regional West Magazine.*

Cobb's work has been exhibited in the U.C. Berkeley Museum at Blackhawk in Danville, California, and the Nevada Museum of Art in Reno, as well as in galleries around California, Florida and Washington, D.C.

Ron Bath

The hands-on woodworker mills his own lumber, preferring to leave the natural edge on boards. With geometric shapes and a variety of woods, he creates striking juxtapositions of form, color and texture. He also experiments by adding other materials such as stone, metal, paint or dye and glass.

"I play with the movement of how drawers open and close, creating a unique kinetic experience," Cobb says. "I rarely repeat a design I have made and I try to go beyond the mundane function of a piece of furniture."

Cobb's Gallery pieces, "Sand Whispers", conjure images of eternal sandscapes frozen in time on the surfaces of pale wood.

Retro Sleek

Jay and Janet O'Rourke

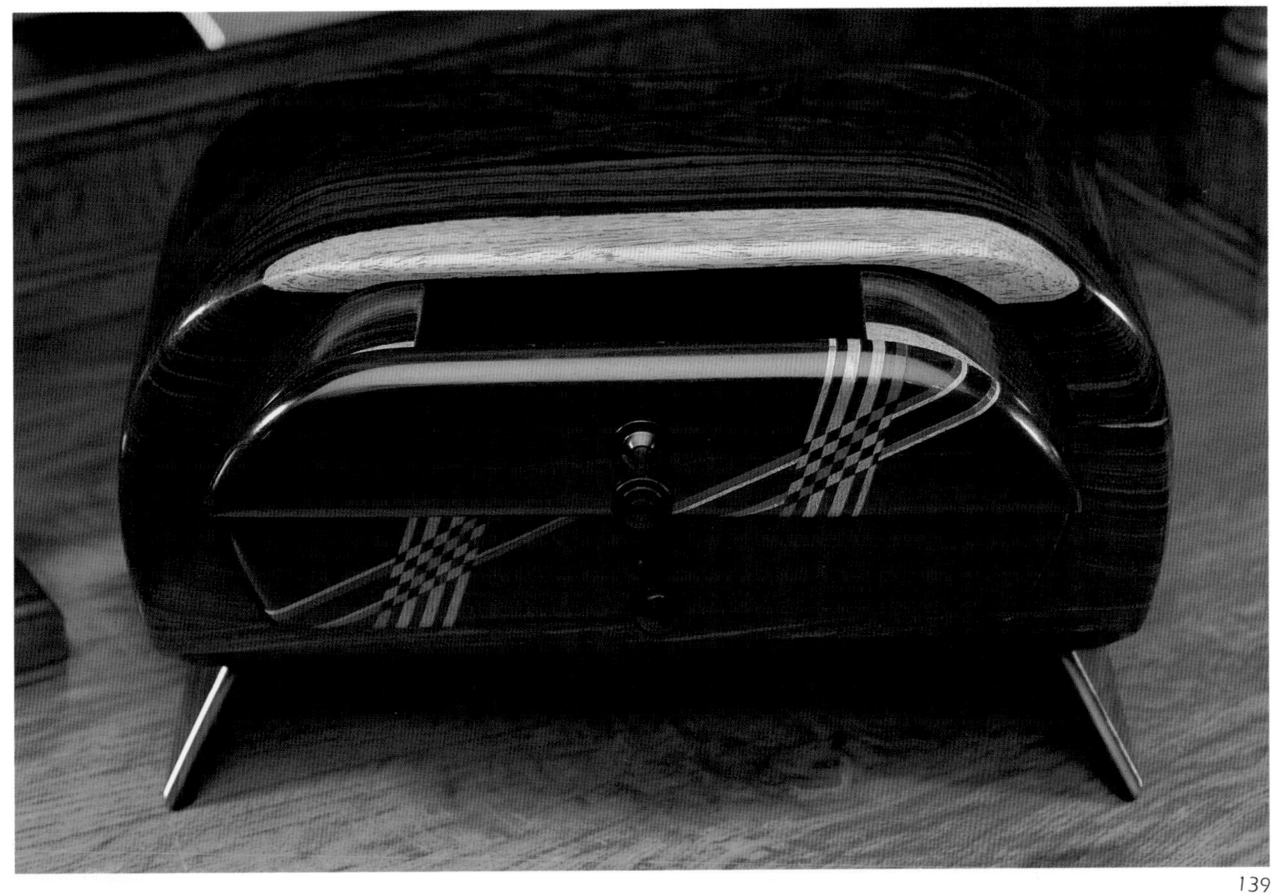

Jay and Janet O'Rourke

The Jay O Box, creation of California natives Jay and Janet O'Rourke, is unique in that the central portion of the box is cut from one hand-shaped piece of wood to which the sides are then laminated.

Jay is a self-taught woodworker who attended Santa Barbara City College. Janet has a fine arts degree from the Academy of Art College in San Francisco, California, and has pursued graduate work at Otis Parsons in Los Angeles.

Jay O'Rourke began crafting wood boxes many years ago for the Renaissance Faire in California. He went on to exhibit at wholesale and retail shows and craft fairs.

Jay O Boxes are featured in over 150 galleries nationwide. They have also appeared in numerous juried shows, such as the Washington Craft Show at The Smithsonian Museum, Washington, D.C. Their work has also been seen in *Southern California Home and Garden* and *American Craft Magazine.*

Striking color combinations of woods and mirror-polished surfaces are hallmarks of the Jay O style. "To us, they are like jewels," Jay says. Adds Janet, "We are inspired by Art Deco and ancient Asian art. We love doing wild laminations and graphic design with all natural wood colors."

"Retro Sleek", the Jay O Box shown in the Gallery, exemplifies the design sense and craftsmanship of the O'Rourkes. Its depth of luster, sleek lines and hint of bamboo pattern evoke both the Art Deco period and the Orient.

Metric Conversion Chart

MM - Millimeters CM - Centimeters

INCHES TO MILLIMETERS AND CENTIMETERS

INCHES	MM	CM	INCHES	CM	INCHES	CM
⅛	3	0.3	9	22.9	30	76.2
¼	6	0.6	10	25.4	31	78.7
⅜	10	1.0	11	27.9	32	81.3
½	13	1.3	12	30.5	33	83.8
⅝	16	1.6	13	33.0	34	86.4
¾	19	1.9	14	35.6	35	88.9
⅞	22	2.2	15	38.1	36	91.4
1	25	2.5	16	40.6	37	94.0
1¼	32	3.2	17	43.2	38	96.5
1½	38	3.8	18	45.7	39	99.1
1¾	44	4.4	19	48.3	40	101.6
2	51	5.1	20	50.8	41	104.1
2½	64	6.4	21	53.3	42	106.7
3	76	7.6	22	55.9	43	109.2
3½	89	8.9	23	58.4	44	111.8
4	102	10.2	24	61.0	45	114.3
4½	114	11.4	25	63.5	46	116.8
5	127	12.7	26	66.0	47	119.4
6	152	15.2	27	68.6	48	121.9
7	178	17.8	28	71.1	49	124.5
8	203	20.3	29	73.7	50	127.0

YARDS TO METERS

Yards	Meters	Yards	Meters	Yards	Meters	Yards	Meters	Yards	Meters
⅛	0.11	2⅛	1.94	4⅛	3.77	6⅛	5.60	8⅛	7.43
¼	0.23	2¼	2.06	4¼	3.89	6¼	5.72	8¼	7.54
⅜	0.34	2⅜	2.17	4⅜	4.00	6⅜	5.83	8⅜	7.66
½	0.46	2½	2.29	4½	4.11	6½	5.94	8½	7.77
⅝	0.57	2⅝	2.40	4⅝	4.23	6⅝	6.06	8⅝	7.89
¾	0.69	2¾	2.51	4¾	4.34	6¾	6.17	8¾	8.00
⅞	0.80	2⅞	2.63	4⅞	4.46	6⅞	6.29	8⅞	8.12
1	0.91	3	2.74	5	4.57	7	6.40	9	8.23
1⅛	1.03	3⅛	2.86	5⅛	4.69	7⅛	6.52	9⅛	8.34
1¼	1.14	3¼	2.97	5¼	4.80	7¼	6.63	9¼	8.46
1⅜	1.26	3⅜	3.09	5⅜	4.91	7⅜	6.74	9⅜	8.57
1½	1.37	3½	3.20	5½	5.03	7½	6.86	9½	8.69
1⅝	1.49	3⅝	3.31	5⅝	5.14	7⅝	6.97	9⅝	8.80
1¾	1.60	3¾	3.43	5¾	5.26	7¾	7.09	9¾	8.92
1⅞	1.71	3⅞	3.54	5⅞	5.37	7⅞	7.20	9⅞	9.03
2	1.83	4	3.66	6	5.49	8	7.32	10	9.14

Index

Boxes

Box-makers

General Instructions / 6 - 19

Metric Conversion Chart / 142